Antique Trader®

Collectible COOKBOOKS

PRICE GUIDE

©2008 Krause Publications

Published by

kp krause publications

An Imprint of F+W Publications

700 East State Street • Iola, WI 54990-0001
715-445-2214 • 888-457-2873
www.krausebooks.com

Our toll-free number to place an order or obtain
a free catalog is (800) 258-0929.

The prices listed in this book are provided only as a guide and not as a listing of any established or set pricing standard. Prices may vary substantially depending on where, when and how books are purchased or sold. Physical condition, market location, availability, dealer versus collector pricing, and auction sale prices can result in a wide range of variability. Every attempt has been made to present both editorial and pricing information as accurately as possible. Neither the authors nor the publisher assume any liability for losses incurred in the purchasing, selling or transaction of any items as a result of the information provided in this book. Readers are encouraged to bring any errors or inaccuracies to our attention at OldCookbooks.com.

Library of Congress Control Number: 2008928403

ISBN-13: 978-0-89689-669-7
ISBN-10: 0-89689-669-2

Designed by Katrina Newby
Edited by Joe Kertzman

Printed in China

Antique Trader®

Collectible COOKBOOKS

PRICE GUIDE

Patricia Edwards ◆ Peter Peckham

More Great Books in the Antique Trader® Series

Contents

Acknowledgements

Our special thanks to:

◆ Kimberly Kaye for her talented research and writing of many of the author introductions.

◆ Lynne Olver at www.foodtimeline.org for her creative and generous research help.

Welcome to the Guide

Whether you're just starting a collection, or are a seasoned connoisseur of culinary literature, you'll find this guide a valuable resource for identifying, pricing and learning about 20th-century American cookbooks published from the late 1800's up to about the 1970s—a rather large slice of publishing history filled with rich examples of culinary art, culture, trends, humor and, of course, recipes for some great food.

As owners of OldCookbooks.com, one of the largest online bookstores specializing in vintage, used and out-of-print cookbooks, and with over 15,000 cookbooks and recipe booklets in our current stock, we have edited our selections, focusing on those titles that have either maintained their popularity or have grown in demand in our experience as vintage cookbook dealers.

In addition to providing estimated market values for hundreds of cookbooks, this guide includes:

◆ Over 800 color photos for easy identification

◆ Interesting tidbits about cookbook authors, publishers and food product companies

◆ Helpful tips for cookbook collecting and care

◆ A handy title index

◆ The basics of how to evaluate and understand cookbook condition

◆ An overview of the qualities that determine a cookbook's desirability and value

About Values

Values found in this guide are estimated retail values, presented as a range of prices based on condition. For example, a value range of $5-$25, would reflect the difference between a book in "okay" condition versus a copy in very good condition.

Advice for Beginning Collectors

Our best advice is probably true for collecting anything—collect what you find interesting, meaningful, fun or important. Let your collection be an expression of your interest, not just the value the marketplace puts on your books.

A Recipe for Success

◆ Try to buy books with dust jackets whenever possible. A dust jacket not only protects the book, but it often provides hard-to-find information about the author or the cookbook itself. Dust jackets are often missing from older cookbooks and, when intact, instantly add value.

◆ Buy the best condition you can afford. Buying a book in "cooking copy" condition is a good idea only if you intend to use it in the kitchen, or consider it a "placeholder" in your collection.

◆ Store your cookbooks out of the kitchen, out of the basement and out of the attic. Even the cleanest kitchens tend to be a challenging environment for a book (grease, smoke, moisture, humidity, etc.) And we've seen a lot of great old books ruined by insects, moisture, heat and other effects of improper storage.

◆ If you intend to use the cookbooks you purchase, consider buying the best copy you can afford and buying another one in marginal shape for the kitchen.

◆ Buy from reputable dealers who know cookbooks, know how to describe them and offer a money-back satisfaction guarantee.

◆ Focus your collection on a particular sub-category or passion. This might be anything from a collection of cookbooks from your region to a collection about confections, cakes or cocktails. From a buyer's point of view, focused and complete collections are more desirable than a disparate gaggle of books. From a collector's perspective, it will make your treasure hunting more manageable.

What Makes a Cookbook Collectible?

It's a question we are often asked, and one for which the answer depends on who's collecting and why. Besides those who just want to find great recipes and make good things to eat, there are those who collect books based on value, and some wanting to preserve or explore a culture, a style or a place. Others just love reading interesting cookbooks (as some do novels).

Collectible is in the eye of the beholder, whereas value, in simple terms, is more a measure of how much one is willing to pay for it.

The special charm of collecting cookbooks is that there is an enormous range of sub-categories of interest, making most cookbooks desirable, though not necessarily valuable. Sprinkled throughout this book you will find ideas and information about collected cookbook categories, things to look for and tips for building an interesting collection.

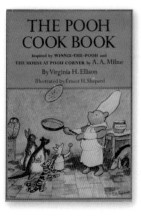

Judging A Book By Its Cover

ANATOMY OF A BOOK

A COVER OR BOARDS

B ENDPAPERS

C FLYLEAF, FIRST FREE ENDPAPER

D FOREDGE

E HINGES

F HEAD OR TOP EDGE

G TAIL OR BOTTOM EDGE

H SPINE

OUTSIDE

INSIDE

Grading and Condition

Throughout their potentially long lives, books experience various kinds of wear and tear that can affect their value. Especially as books age, a variety of conditional issues may begin to appear, such as the damaging effects of dust, moisture, oxidation, mold and mildew. Original printing/binding quality and the care with which various owners handled and stored a book can make a significant difference in condition as it ages.

Assigning the condition to a cookbook is called grading. Book dealers use a shorthand system and many terms that might be foreign to the uninitiated. We use a simpler system on our website, grading a book's condition from A to F. See the chart below to familiarize yourself with the categories of condition.

Keep in mind that the older the book, the more lenient the grading—a book described as "Very Good" with a pub date of 2005 should be an extremely nice, lightly used copy, but a cookbook described as "Very Good" with a pub date of 1910 is likely to have heavier wear. In addition, the type of book will affect the grading. For example, as a result of the way they are used, more flaws are expected in children's books, instruction manuals and cookbooks.

Categories of Condition*

Fine or Near Fine, As New, Near New, Like New
Appears unused, but may be previously owned.

Very Good
Less than perfect, may show normal wear for its age or type.

Good
Obviously used, showing heavier wear for its age and type. No defects affecting overall structure, but may have cosmetic flaws, repairs etc.

Fair or "Cooking Copies"
More wear and damage (stains, bumps, repairs, minor tears, etc.) but intact and functional.

Poor
Could have any number of serious defects, including missing pages.

*Terms may be abbreviated (e.g. "VG/G," which indicates that the book is in very good condition and the dust jacket is in good condition.) A plus or minus sign may also be added to this (as VG+), indicating it is slightly better or slightly worse than the indicated grade. This abbreviated note is usually followed by further description of various possible problems.

What Is It Worth?

A variety of factors can affect the value of a collectible cookbook. Values are subject to cooking trends, time of year and even media exposure. Several years ago, the *New York Times* ran a short article mentioning the 1959 *Pillsbury 1000 Best of the Bake-off Cookbook*. Overnight auction prices for this particular book rose tenfold. Conversely, the original 1950 *Betty Crocker's Picture Cook Book* was reprinted in the 1990s, causing values for the original printing to noticeably decline.

Use this guide as a compass to direct you, but not as a bible. There are thousands and thousands of additional cookbooks and recipe booklets that are collected, and the complexity of the market and of the subject make definitive pricing impossible. Scarcity, popularity and age are just a few essential ingredients affecting value.

Here are some additional factors that affect cookbook values shown in the guide:

◆ *Dust jacket.* Even a worn dust jacket can add significant value to the cookbook. It is protective and informative, offering clues to the edition, author's biography and historical significance—add 10%-30% to the high-end value of the book.

◆ *Author signature.* Signed cookbook values are subject to the public whim, but as a rule of thumb, multiply the highest value by three to six times for authors who are relatively famous and deceased. Signatures by lesser-known authors generally do not add to the value of the cookbook.

◆ *Handwritten recipes.* Notes and recipes, as well as previous owner names or bookplates, add a sense of personality and provenance and can add value. This is a bit subjective and may include factors such as the owner's handwriting, date of the cookbook, and the quantity and quality of recipes. As a general rule, add 10%-30% if the recipes and handwriting are legible and plentiful.

◆ *Missing pages.* If the cookbook is missing pages, but rare, subtract at least 50% from the lowest value given in the guide. Any cookbook that is easily found or printed after about 1910 with missing pages will generally be considered of little or no value.

◆ *Heavy damage.* Food soiling, torn pages, insect or other noticeable damage is forgivable in rare cases, but generally affects value considerably. Subtract at least 50% from low-end price.

There are still many affordable and undiscovered treasures, so get out there and shop!

A Word About Repairs
Should you repair it, or leave it alone?

A rule of thumb—if it is a cookbook you use and if the item is likely to become more damaged without a repair, a repair is acceptable. For example, a weak binding that is about to break or a badly torn page could benefit by spare and neat use of archival tapes (that won't yellow, crack or ooze). That being said, benign neglect (do nothing) is the best policy. We recommend that rare cookbooks, or books you are collecting for value, be repaired professionally or not at all.

Chapter 1: *General Cookbooks*

This chapter is devoted to commercially produced cookbooks, and organized alphabetically by author (or publisher if no author noted), allowing you to see at a glance what cookbooks were written by a particular author. Hundreds of cookbooks are covered, with an emphasis on titles from the mid-20th century. Coverage ends around 1970 except where desirable to round out or complete an author listing. While this guide is not a complete listing of all the collectible or desirable cookbooks from this period, it is a solid survey of the famous and the favorites, as well as some of the odd and the obscure.

If you are new to collecting, this chapter will familiarize you with popular and interesting collectibles, and help you to develop your instinct for what is worth buying or collecting. If you are already a collector, we hope the author research, value guidelines and tips will enhance the enjoyment of your collection.

Allen, Ida Bailey

The original domestic goddess, America's Mrs. Allen, nee Ida Cogswell, was born in 1885 and has been credited with bringing nutrition, world cuisine and formal cooking to thousands of average housewives (it is also said that she invented the marshmallow-topped sweet potato casserole). An avid cook, "domestic science" professional and a practicing dietitian, she was the first woman in history to bring food to the masses using all available media outlets: in print, as the author of over 50 cookbooks, including *The Best Loved Recipes of the American People*, and as a contributor to over half dozen major magazines (*Good Housekeeping, Parade*); on the radio, as the host of a popular radio show; and on TV, acting as television's first female food host on *Mrs. Allen and the Chef*.

Confessing that the radio was "a fearsome thing," she nevertheless went on to pioneer a popular radio show for homemakers and founded the "National Radio Homemaker's Club," which surprised her with its overwhelming success and delighted her with the way it united women while they "kept house." Her power to influence was demonstrated one Christmas when she suggested that women could wear red Christmas dresses to please their children, and stores reported a surge in requests for red holiday garb.

Mrs. Allen was also the queen of the sensible kitchen, penning some of the first books dedicated solely to budget cuisine, cooking for two and efficient timesaving meals.

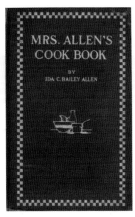

1917
Mrs. Allen's Cook Book
Allen, Ida Bailey
Small, Maynard and Co.
Hardcover
756 pages plus ads
14 pages of ads and additional "memoranda" pages. Black and white photos
Value: $16-$28

1926
104 Prize Radio Recipes
Allen, Ida Bailey
J. H. Sears & Co.
Hardcover
126 pages
A series of 24 radio addresses by Allen are reproduced here with the recipe contest prize-winning recipes. Illustrative look at how radio shows shaped the thinking of the American homemaker
Value: $31-$56

1927
Modern Method Of Preparing Delightful Foods, The
Allen, Ida Bailey
Corn Products Refining Co.
Hardcover
109 pages plus index
Compelling writings on historical American cooking in colonial times. Includes a photo of Mrs. Allen. Promotes cooking with Karo Syrup, Kingsford Cornstarch and Mazola Oil
Value: $19-$34

1933
Service Cook Book Number One, The
Allen, Ida Bailey
Service, Inc.
Hardcover
Un-paginated. Published exclusively for F.W. Woolworth Co. Full-page photo of Mrs. Ida Bailey Allen
Value: $12-$22

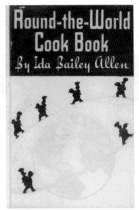

1934
Round-The-World Cook Book
Allen, Ida Bailey
Best Foods
Hardcover
96 pages
Recipes call for Nucoa margarine.
Value: $9-$16

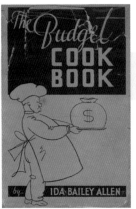

1935
Budget Cook Book, The
Allen, Ida Bailey
The Best Foods, Inc.
Hardcover
128 pages
Recipes call for Nucoa margarine. Dust jacket cover shows ad for Nucoa.
Value: $9-$16

1940
Ida Bailey Allen's Money-Saving Cook Book
Allen, Ida Bailey
Garden City Publishing
Hardcover
481 pages
Value: $16-$28

1947
Food For Two
Allen, Ida Bailey
Garden City
Hardcover
339 pages
Value: $25-$44

1952
Ida Bailey Allen's Step-By-Step Picture Cook Book
Allen, Ida Bailey
Grosset & Dunlap
Hardcover
248 pages
Color and black-and-white photos
Value: $11-$19

1957
Ida Bailey Allen's Cook Book For Two
Allen, Ida Bailey
Doubleday
Hardcover
Revised edition of the earlier *Food for Two*
Value: $4-$7

Ashley, Roberta

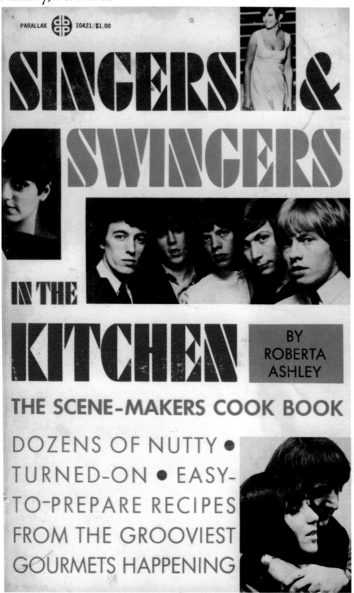

1967
Singers And Swingers In The Kitchen
Ashley, Roberta
Parallax
Soft cover
96 pages
Favorite recipes of '60s pop idols like Sonny and Cher, The Monkees, The Hermits, The Rolling Stones, Bobby Darin and many more. Black and white photos of celebrities throughout
Value: $60-$106

Aunt Sammy

A unt Sammy was the fictional spouse of the equally fictional Uncle Sam, and an idealized homebody who personalized the nutritional messages from the U.S. Government. The real Aunt Sammys who offered household advice and recipes via the radio show *Housekeeper's Chat* were local home economists.

The most popular recipes from the show were compiled into the *Aunt Sammy's Radio Recipes* cookbook to meet the clamoring demand of show listeners. Enlarged and revised several times, it holds the distinction of being the first cookbook produced in Braille.

Barber, Edith M.

1931
Aunt Sammy's Radio Recipes Revised
Van Deman, Ruth
Bureau of Home Economics, U.S. Department of Agriculture
Soft cover
142 pages
Collection of 400 of the most popular recipes and 90 menus from the 1926 radio program *Housekeeper's Chats* produced by the Bureau of Home Economics
Value: $13-$24

1950
Spice Sampler, The
Barber, Edith M.
Sterling Publishing
Hardcover
62 pages
Includes spice sample packets from John Wagner & Sons of Hatboro, Pa.
Cloth cover
Value: $27-$48

Batchelder, Ann

Hearty Vermonter with an unpretentious upbringing and a self-described adventurer, a suffragette and lover of books and food all combine to make up the portrait of Batchelder, who we imagine would be played by Katherine Hepburn. From a stint at the *Delineator Magazine*, she eventually found her way to become a popular food editor for *Ladies' Home Journal*.

A frank and friendly self-portrait of Batchelder's life can be found in her personal cookbook *Ann Batchelder's Own Cook Book*, wherein she recounts life lessons and her ideals alongside recipes for Sweet Potato Pumpkins and Shrewsbury Cakes.

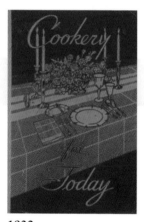

1932
Cookery For Today
Batchelder, Ann
Butterick
Hardcover
164 pages
Black and white photos and illustrations
Value: $6-$10

1941
Ann Batchelder's Own Cook Book
Batchelder, Ann
M. Barrows & Co.
Hardcover
232 pages
Personal cookbook written in witty, conversational style with personal anecdotes and history
Value: $17-$31

Bazore, Katherine

1967
Hawaiian And Pacific Foods
Bazore, Katherine
Gramercy
Hardcover
290 pages
Recipes and customs of the Hawaiian, Samoan, Chinese, Japanese and Filipino
Value: $13-$23

Beard, James

An opera singer and radio personality, Beard ultimately found his calling when he (along with friend Bill Rhodes) created the New York catering company, Hors D'Oeuvre, Inc., which profited from the 1930s cocktail party phenomenon. Specializing in creating the New York cocktail party and supper, the popularity of his food and entertaining skills led to his first cookbook *Hors D'Oeuvre and Canapés*. His subsequent 1946 TV cooking show *I Love to Eat* was billed as "the first show of its type."

Beard's cookbooks number over 20, about half of which are still in print. Today the James Beard Foundation (at www.JamesBeard.org) champions his legacy and promotes culinary excellence through workshops and scholarships.

1940
Hors D'oeuvres And Canapes With A Key To The Cocktail Party
Beard, James
M. Barrows & Co.
Hardcover
190 pages
Beard's first book. Black-and-white photos
Value: $25-$44

1941, 1946
Cook It Outdoors
Beard, James
M. Barrows & Co.
Hardcover
200 pages
Outdoor recipes include Fuddy Duddy Salad and Nancy Dorris' Salt Pork Dinner.
Value: $24-$43

1949
Fireside Cook Book, The
Beard, James
Simon and Schuster
Hardcover
Illustrations by Alice and Martin Provensen
Value: $48-$86

1949
Fowl And Game Cookery
Beard, James
Blue Ribbon Books
Hardcover
196 pages
Value: $25-$44

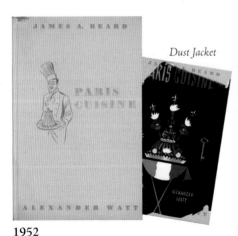

Dust Jacket

1952
Paris Cuisine
Beard, James; Watt, Alexander
Little, Brown & Co.
Hardcover
272 pages
Endpapers show French restaurant menus. Design and
illustrations by Vladimir Bobri
Value: $46-$81

1954
Jim Beard's Complete Party Cookbook
Beard, James
Maco
Soft cover
144 pages
2nd printing of the *Cookbook for Entertaining*
Value: $20-$36

1960
James Beard's Treasury Of Outdoor Cooking
Beard, James
Golden Press
Hardcover
282 pages
Color and black-and-white photos and illustrations
Value: $24-$43

1961
James Beard Cookbook, The
Beard, James and Callvert, Isabel E.
E. P. Dutton
Hardcover
456 pages
Value: $9-$16

1965
James Beard's Menus For Entertaining
Beard, James
Delacorte
Hardcover
398 pages
Value: $11-$19

DEFINITION

Inscribed: refers to the penning of a gift note by previous owner or author. "Previous owner inscribed" is generally considered a negative in book collection, but in older cookbooks can be considered part of the provenance (or history) of the book. It does not generally detract from value, especially in older cookbooks.

Beck, Phineas

1943-1957
Clementine In The Kitchen
Beck, Phineas
Hastings House
Hardcover
228 pages
Vignettes by Henry Stahlhut
Value: $7-$12

Beck, Simone

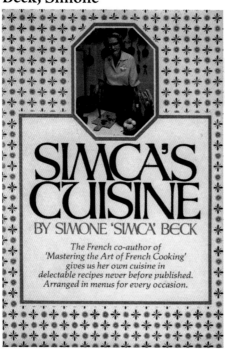

1972
Simca's Cuisine
Beck, Simone and Simon, Patricia
Knopf
Hardcover
326 pages
Illustrations by John Wallner
Value: $11-$19

Berg, Gertrude

1955-1965
Molly Goldberg Jewish Cookbook, The
Berg, Gertrude and Waldo, Myra
Pyramid or Doubleday
Paperback or Hardcover
192 pages
Molly Goldberg is the pseudonym of author Gertrude Berg.
Hardback $40-$50
Paperback shown
Value: $20-$36

Berolzheimer, Ruth

Equal parts accomplished and elusive, the editor, wordsmith and child welfare advocate, Ruth Berolzheimer, was best known as the director of the important Culinary Arts Institute's Culinary Arts Press, a prolific publisher of cookery books. Though the role of director was not clearly defined, Ruth's name was listed as the editor of over 60 publications produced by the company during her employment, which began in 1939 and ended in the 1950s.

Her primary expertise may have been her marketing prowess, contributing to the success of the Culinary Arts Press by recycling recipes and cookbooks, many morphing by name, cover color or sponsor alone.

Her elusiveness comes from a notable lack of biographical background; very little has been written about her life or education, though she clearly was a significant contributor to cookery books during the 1940s. Even more puzzling, her obituary listed in the *New York Times* in 1965 billed her as the author of the well-known *Settlement Cookbook*, despite the fact that the book was actually written by Lizzie Black Kander and assorted assistants.

Collecting cookbooks by Ruth Berolzheimer may turn out to be a full-time endeavor and our list continues to grow.

Look for these additional bindings of *The American Woman's Cook Book*:
Woman's World Binding
International Binding
Everywoman's Binding
See also: Cookbooks: Penny, Prudence.

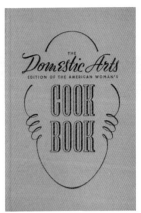

1939
Domestic Arts Edition Of The American Woman's Cook Book
Berolzheimer, Ruth (editor)
Consolidated Book Publishers
Hardcover
815 pages plus an Un-paginated chapter entitled *Cooking for Fifty*
The American Woman's Cook Book, a thick and thorough domestic bible, was printed with many different covers and titles, most with identical contents.
Thumb-indexed
Speckled edge decoration. Black-and-white and color photos
Value: $88-$157

1939-1946
American Woman's Cook Book, The
Berolzheimer, Ruth (editor)
Consolidated Book Publishers
Hardcover
815 pages
From the *Delineator Cook Book*. Edited and revised by Ruth Berolzheimer. All printings with this cover have the same contents with the exception that war years have an additional wartime cookery section at back of book.
Thumb-indexed
Value: $33-$58

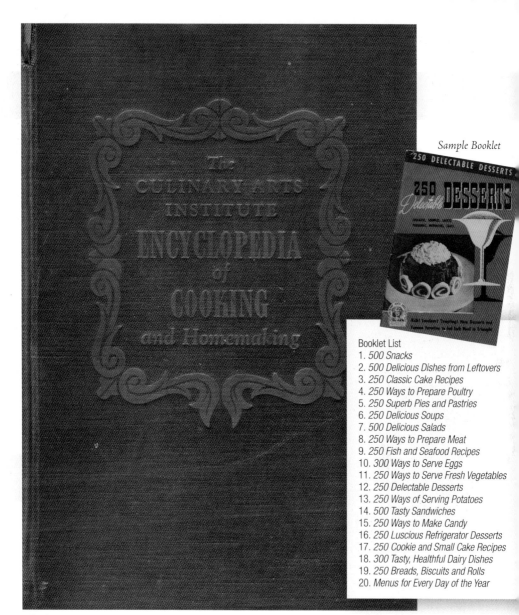

Sample Booklet

Booklet List
1. *500 Snacks*
2. *500 Delicious Dishes from Leftovers*
3. *250 Classic Cake Recipes*
4. *250 Ways to Prepare Poultry*
5. *250 Superb Pies and Pastries*
6. *250 Delicious Soups*
7. *500 Delicious Salads*
8. *250 Ways to Prepare Meat*
9. *250 Fish and Seafood Recipes*
10. *300 Ways to Serve Eggs*
11. *250 Ways to Serve Fresh Vegetables*
12. *250 Delectable Desserts*
13. *250 Ways of Serving Potatoes*
14. *500 Tasty Sandwiches*
15. *250 Ways to Make Candy*
16. *250 Luscious Refrigerator Desserts*
17. *250 Cookie and Small Cake Recipes*
18. *300 Tasty, Healthful Dairy Dishes*
19. *250 Breads, Biscuits and Rolls*
20. *Menus for Every Day of the Year*

1940s
Culinary Arts Institute Encyclopedia Of Cooking And Homemaking, The
Berolzheimer, Ruth (editor)
Culinary Arts Institute
Hardcover binder and 20 booklets
48 pages
Each booklet was printed in a variety of possible colors, including red, green, orange, aqua and blue. The binder is brown with removable binding wires. Individual booklet prices range from $7-$15. Binder is difficult to find in acceptable condition. Also look for the companion box containing the entire set titled *American Encyclopedia of Cooking and Homemaking*. Note that binder must be in exceptional condition to command these prices.
Value: $102-$181

General Douglas MacArthur Illustration

1942, 1943
Victory Binding Of The American Woman's Cook Book Wartime Edition
Berolzheimer, Ruth (editor)
Culinary Arts
Hardcover
816 pages plus wartime section
Printed in 1942 and 1943. The 1943 printing is more desirable and contains a full-page illustration and dedication to Gen. Douglas MacArthur. Both printings have 816 pages plus additional sections devoted to "Wartime Cookery."
Thumb-indexed. Color and black and white photos and illustrations
Value: $88-$156

Dust Jacket

1946-1949
American Woman's Cook Book, The
Berolzheimer, Ruth (editor)
Culinary Arts Institute
Hardcover
824 pages
Cover colors vary, but contents are identical if page count is the same.
Thumb-indexed. Color and black-and-white photos and illustrations
Value: $29-$53

1948
Culinary Arts Institute Encyclopedic Cookbook
Berolzheimer, Ruth (editor)
Culinary Arts Institute
Hardcover
966 pages plus index
Especially desirable version with directions for making a root cellar, a food dryer and a smokehouse
Thumb-indexed
Value: $55-$98

1950-1960s
American Woman's Cook Book, The
Berolzheimer, Ruth (editor)
Garden City
Hardcover
856 pages
Reprinted many times, any date with this cover design has identical contents.
Color and black and white photos and illustrations
Thumb-indexed
Value: $33-$58

CONDITION TIP

Lace-like damage, holes or chewed corners and edges are likely caused by insects like silverfish, worms or hungry rodents using the book for food or shelter. Food stains may attract insects. If you buy a book with insect damage, be sure to lightly vacuum and thoroughly wipe it clean before storing it with other books.

Sample Booklet

1950s

Encyclopedia Of Cooking In 24 Volumes, The

Berolzheimer, Ruth
Culinary Arts Institute
Hardcover binder and 24 booklets
White binder has gold lettering and removable binding
wires. Some binders include index on the spine. Binder is
difficult to find in acceptable condition. Note: binder must be
in exceptional condition to command these prices.
Individual booklet prices range from $3-$15.
Value: $126-$225

Booklet List
1. *500 Snacks—Bright Ideas for Entertaining*
2. *500 Delicious Dinners from Leftovers*
3. *250 Classic Cake Recipes*
4. *250 Ways to Prepare Poultry and Game Birds*
5. *250 Superb Pies and Pastries*
6. *500 Delicious Soup Recipes*
7. *500 Delicious Salad Recipes*
8. *250 Ways to Prepare Meat*
9. *250 Fish and Sea Food Recipes*
10. *300 Ways to Serve Eggs*
11. *250 Ways to Serve Fresh Vegetables*
12. *250 Delectable Dessert Recipes*
13. *250 Ways of Serving Potatoes*
14. *500 Tasty Sandwich Recipes*
15. *250 Ways to Make Candy*
16. *250 Luscious Refrigerator Desserts*
17. *The Cookie Book*
18. *300 Healthful Dairy Dishes*
19. *250 Breads, Biscuits and Rolls*
20. *250 Sauces, Gravies and Dressings*
21. *Meals for Two Cookbook*
22. *Body Building Dishes for Children*
23. *2,000 Useful Facts About Food*
24. *Menus for Every Day of the Year*

1952 & 1947
Kenmore Binding Of The American Woman's Cook Book And The United States Regional Cook Book
Berolzheimer, Ruth (editor)
Culinary Arts Institute
Hardcover
846 pages and 752 pages
The two-volume set, in slipcase, is a promotional set of the *American Woman's Cook Book* and the *United States Regional Cook Book* bound for Sears Roebuck.
Color and black and white photos
Thumb-indexed
Value: $88-$156

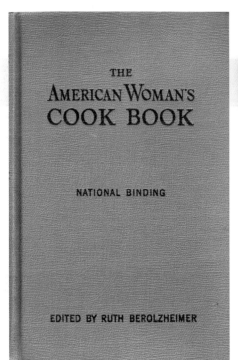

DEFINITION

Slipcase: a cardboard open-ended box cover used to protect a single volume or set of books.

1955
American Woman's Cook Book, The
Berolzheimer, Ruth (editor)
Culinary Arts Institute
Hardcover
856 pages
Aqua-blue or mint-green National Binding
New and revised edition. Thumb-indexed
Aqua cover 1947-1950s
Value: $30-$53

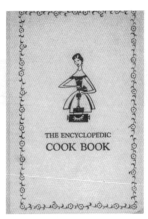

1958
Encyclopedic Cook Book, The
Berolzheimer, Ruth (editor)
Culinary Arts Institute
Hardcover
974 pages
New 1958 edition. Thumb-indexed
Value: $27-$48

1958-1976
Culinary Arts Institute Encyclopedic Cookbook New Revised Edition
Berolzheimer, Ruth (editor)
Culinary Arts Institute
Hardcover
974 pages
New Revised Edition
Value: $41-$74

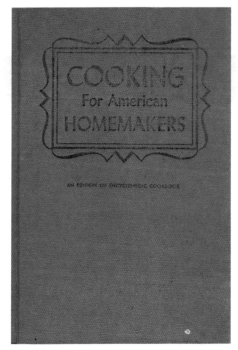

1965
Cooking For American Homemakers
Berolzheimer, Ruth (editor)
Culinary Arts
Hardcover
974 pages
Thick and thorough cookbook reprinted many times with different covers and titles. This is the *Cooking for American Homemakers* cover, but the contents are the same as the other *New Revised Culinary Arts Encyclopedic Cookbooks* of this era.
Color and black and white photos and illustrations
Thumb-indexed
Value: $42-$74

1972

American Woman's Cook Book, The

Berolzheimer, Ruth (editor)
Doubleday & Co.
Hardcover
856 pages plus photos
Not thumb-indexed
Plain forest-green cover
Color and black-and-white photos and illustrations
Value: $28-$50

COLLECTING TIP

The challenge with oversize binder cookbooks is finding binders in good condition. The bindings suffer from the weight of the book and are often excessively worn and/or torn. A high-quality repair with archival tapes is considered acceptable and will keep the binder from deteriorating further.

Alternate Cover, Same Contents

1947

United States Regional Cook Book, The

Berolzheimer, Ruth (editor)
Culinary Arts Institute
Hardcover
752 pages
Etchings and jacket by Albert H. Winkler. Also published as *The Greater American Cook Book*. Thumb-indexed
Cover colors and fabric type vary, but contents are identical.
Value: $33-$69

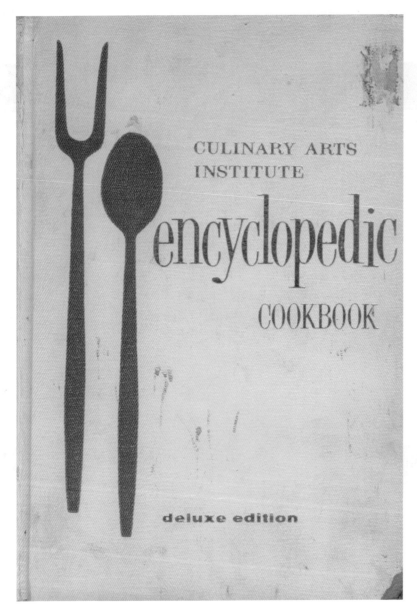

1959-1974
Culinary Arts Institute Encyclopedic Cookbook
Berolzheimer, Ruth (editor)
Culinary Arts Institute
Hardcover
974 plus index
New Revised Edition
Value: $23-$42

Better Homes and Gardens

Better Homes and Gardens' roots travel back to the 1920s, when Iowan founder E.T. Meredith produced *Fruit, Garden and Home*, a practical magazine with recipes and tips for gardening and decorating. Re-titled *Better Homes and Gardens* in 1924, the magazine included a section featuring recipes submitted by readers called "Cook's Round Table."

From this column emerged Better Homes and Garden's first cook booklet *The 202 Best and Most Interesting Recipes from Cooks' Round Table*, a compilation of collected recipes that today is difficult to find and could fetch from $30-$100.

Along with the growing success and readership of *Better Homes and Gardens*, the popularity of recipes continued. Soon a test kitchen was built and staffed with home economic professionals hired to judge, test and revise recipes to make them easy to follow and understand.

One of the most successful examples of cookbook branding is the enduring *Better Homes and Gardens Cookbook* with its red-plaid cover introduced in 1941. It continues, after more than 60 years of subsequent editions, to be one of the most memorable and recognizable cookbooks today.

My
BETTER HOMES
AND GARDENS
COOK BOOK

•

EVERY RECIPE TESTED
IN THE
BETTER HOMES AND GARDENS
TASTING-TEST KITCHEN

1933-1936
My Better Homes And Gardens Cook Book
Better Homes and Gardens
Meredith Publishing
Hardcover binder
Silver binder with black tabs. Complete with table of contents half-card at front of binder, envelope and half-card at back
Value: $32-$56

DEFINITION

Binder: A set of three- or five-hole rings holding a set of loose pages together (like a notebook). Also called "loose leaf", "ring-bound" and erroneously "spiral bound." Sometimes used to refer to other types of special binding that allows removal of booklets or pages.

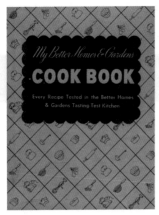

1938
My Better Homes & Gardens Cook Book
Editors of *Better Homes and Gardens*
Better Homes and Gardens
Hardcover binder
Value: $25-$44

1941-1946
Better Homes And Gardens Cook Book De Luxe Edition
Editors of *Better Homes and Gardens*
Better Homes
Hardcover
Blue tabs are lettered. DeLuxe Edition
Value: $23-$41

1944
Better Homes & Gardens Cook Book
Better Homes and Gardens
Meredith
Hardcover binder
The desirable wartime edition of the *Better Homes and Gardens DeLuxe Edition Cook Book*, complete with the *Wartime Supplement* in separate wrapper
Black-and-white and color photos
Blue tabs with lettered indexing
Value: $69-$123

1947-1951
Better Homes And Gardens Cook Book Revised Deluxe Edition
Editors of *Better Homes and Gardens*
Meredith
Hardcover binder
Revised DeLuxe Edition. Blue numbered tabs
Value: $27-$58

1953
Better Homes And Gardens New Cook Book
Editors of *Better Homes and Gardens*
Meredith Publishing
Hardcover binder
Pink tabs with black-and-white illustrations
Color and black-and-white photos, with illustrations throughout
Value: $34-$61

1955
Better Homes And Gardens Junior Cook Book
Editors of *Better Homes and Gardens*
Meredith
Hardcover
Also available as a binder. Color and black-and-white photos and illustrations
Value: $13-$23

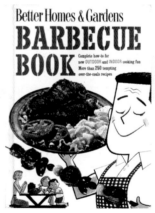

1959
Better Homes & Gardens Barbecue Book
Editors of *Better Homes and Gardens*
Meredith
Hardcover
162 pages
Value: $14-$24

1960-1970
**Better Homes And Gardens
Dessert Cook Book**
Editors of *Better Homes and Gardens*
Meredith publishing
Hardcover
160 pages
Color and black-and-white photos and illustrations
Value: $11-$19

1961
**Better Homes And Gardens New
Cook Book Souvenir Edition**
Editors of *Better Homes and Gardens*
Meredith Publishing
Hardcover
400 pages
Commemorating the sale of 10 million *Better Homes and
Gardens New Cookbooks*
Same contents as 1962 red plaid binder
Yellow tabs
Value: $39-$69

1962-1965
**Better Homes And Gardens New
Cook Book**
Editors of *Better Homes and Gardens*
Meredith Publishing
Hardcover binder
Yellow tabs
Value: $41-$73

1965
**Better Homes And Gardens
Barbecue Book**
Editors of *Better Homes and Gardens*
Meredith Press
Hardcover
Prolifically illustrated with stylized period illustrations and
photos depicting the happy, post-war outdoor lifestyle
Value: $11-$19

Boothby, Hon. Wm. T.

1934
Cocktail Bill Boothby's World Drinks And How To Mix Them
Boothby, Hon. Wm. T.
Boothby's World Drinks
Soft cover
270 pages
Value: $326-$581

Botsford, Harry

1952
Elsie's Cook Book
Botsford, Harry and Elsie the Cow
Bond Wheelwright
Hardcover
374 pages
Illustrations by Keith Ward
Value: $25-$44

Bracken, Peg

As a working mom in the '60s, Bracken struggled along with her female coworkers and friends to balance home and work. The result was several comedic books in the "I Hate to ..." series. The refreshing look at the challenges of housework for a working woman presents her angst with a frank humor that is still hilarious.

The original *I Hate to Cook Book* manuscript—a truly funny and revealing look at the changing domestic roles of American women, as well as a collection of easy recipes—was turned down by many male editors who worried it would offend women. It went on to sell over 3 million copies. Sassy and smart, Bracken's cookbooks are destined for the collector's shelf.

Advertising executive, copywriter and self-described humorist, Bracken died recently at the age of 89.

1962
I Hate To Housekeep Book, The
Bracken, Peg
Harcourt, Brace and World, Inc.
Hardcover, but also available in paperback
176 pages
Illustrations by Hilary Knight
Value: $25-$44

1963
I Hate To Cook Book, The
Bracken, Peg
Harcourt, Brace
Hardcover, but also available in paperback
176 pages
Illustrations by Hilary Knight
Value: $32-$56

1966
Peg Bracken's Appendix To The I Hate To Cook Book
Bracken, Peg
Harcourt Brace and World
Hardcover, but also available in paperback
179 pages
A sequel to *I Hate to Cook Book* with more charming illustrations by Hilary Knight
140 recipes and 323 afterthoughts
Value: $18-$31

Bradley, Alice

1927
Electric Refrigerator Recipes And Menus
Bradley, Alice
General Electric
Hardcover
Value: $12-$21

Brobeck, Florence

A world traveler, Brobeck's many best-selling cookbooks reflect her love of aromatic and ethnic cooking. She wrote a popular weekly column for the *New York Times* and was a contributing food writer to major publications, including the *New Yorker* and *Good Housekeeping*.

1953
Old-Time Pickling And Spicing Recipes
Brobeck, Florence
Gramercy Publishing
Hardcover
126 pages
Value: $22-$39

1955
New Cook It In A Casserole, The
Brobeck, Florence
Barrows & Co.
Hardcover
256 pages
Value: $6-$10

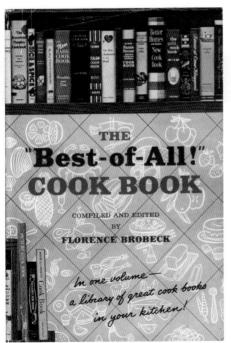

1960
Best-Of-All! Cook Book
Brobeck, Florence
Kingston House
Hardcover
512 pages
Color photos
Value: $25-$44

Brown, Cora, Rose and Bob

A trio of food-savvy familial writers, the Browns spent roughly 20 years writing over a dozen guides to food, wine and spirits. A traveler by nature and college dropout, Robert "Bob" Carlton Brown II left the United States in 1913 with his first wife, Lillian Fox, to see the world and write. After seven years of marriage and frequent moves, Bob and Lillian divorced, and Bob returned to New York to open a restaurant.

Shortly thereafter he married his second wife, Rose Watson, who took to his traveling and shared his love of food and drink. In 1932 Bob penned *Let There Be Beer!*, an amusing guide to the history of beer and his first attempt in the food writing genre.

Encouraged by this venture, Bob was joined by his mother, Cora, and Rose for the second attempt, *The Wine Cook Book* (1934). Praised by critics, the book solidified their partnership, and the three worked closely together to produce nine more cookbooks, before Cora's death in 1939.

Other cookbooks by the Brown trio:

1940: *America Cooks: Favorite Recipes from the 48 States*
1938: *Most for Your Money Cookbook*
1939: *The South American Cook Book*

After Rose's death, Bob and his third wife, Eleanor, collaborated to produce the invaluable *Culinary Americana* (1961), a century's worth of American cookbook bibliographies.

1937-1948
10,000 Snacks
Brown, Cora; Brown, Rose; and Brown, Bob
Halcyon House
Hardcover
593 pages
10,000 or so recipes presented in an appealing and conversational style
Value: $13-$23

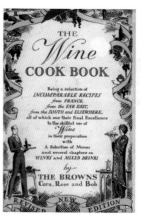

1941
Wine Cook Book, The
Brown, Cora; Brown, Rose; and Brown, Bob
Little, Brown & Co.
Hardcover
462 pages
Recipes organized by type of wine or alcoholic ingredients used. Additional chapters about wines, cocktails, liqueurs, etc. The *Chicago Tribune* called it " glorious collection of inspirations, wise warnings, gay anecdotes and season advice concerning the art of preparing noble dishes and nobler drinks."
Revised edition shown
Value: $25-$44

Brown, Helen Evans

Author, editor, food consultant and talented cook, Helen Evans Brown was one of the authoritative culinary voices during the 1950s and '60s. A former caterer and restaurateur, Helen followed love to the West Coast and was soon hired as a consultant in Hollywood. Her first book, *The Chafing Dish Book* (1950), led to a lucrative food-writing career, as well as other popular cookbooks such as *The Complete Book of Outdoor Cookery* (written with James Beard) and *The West Coast Cook Book*, the latter of which is considered the definitive guide to West Coast cuisine and cookery.

She was widely considered the next in line to succeed Jane Nickerson after her departure as *The New York Times'* food editor, and longtime friend James Beard (as well as Nickerson) voiced displeasure when Craig Claiborne was chosen instead. Beard and Helen were so close, in fact, that a book of their written platonic correspondence with one another was published under the title *James Beard: Love and Kisses and a Halo of Truffles: Letters to Helen Evans Brown.*

Helen herself loved cookbooks, and amassed an impressive collection of thousands over several decades.

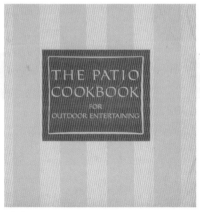

1951
Patio Cookbook For Outdoor Entertaining, The
Brown, Helen Evans
Ward Ritchie Press
Soft cover
141 pages
Value: $5-$8

1952
Helen Brown's West Coast Cook Book
Brown, Helen Evans
Little, Brown and Co.
Hardcover
Value: $10-$18

1953
Virginia City Cook Book, The
Brown, Helen Evans; Brown, Philip S.; Best, Katharine; and Hillyer,
Katharine
Ward Ritchie Press
Hardcover
148 pages
Appealing graphic design by Ward Ritchie with engravings by Harry O. Diamond
Value: $19-$33

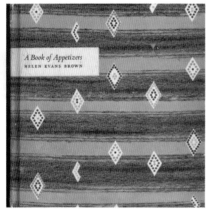

1958
Book Of Appetizers, A
Brown, Helen Evans
Ward Ritchie Press
Hardcover
Originally printed in 1950. Shown is the 1958 reprint available as a three-volume set with slipcase accompanied by *Patio Cook Book* and *Chafing Dish Book*.
Price shown for individual volume. Set is approximately $20-$30.
Value: $6-$11

1958
Chafing Dish Book
Brown, Helen Evans
Ward Ritchie Press
Hardcover
Originally printed in 1950. Shown is the 1958 reprint available as a three-volume set with slipcase accompanied by *Patio Cook Book* and *A Book of Appetizers*. Price shown for individual volume. Set is approximately $20-$30.
Value: $6-$11

1959
Boys' Cook Book, The
Brown, Helen Evans
Doubleday
Hardcover
285 pages
Shown is a less desirable 1970s reprint. Illustrations by
Harry O. Diamond
Value: $13-$23

Brown, Marion

1951-1956
Southern Cook Book, The
Brown, Marion
Pocket
Paperback
414 pages
Value: $6-$10

Butterick Publishing

1929
New Delineator Recipes
Author not noted
Butterick Publishing
Hardcover
222 pages
Shown is the brown cloth cover with yellow/green decorations.
Recipes and table service instructions. Black-and-white photos
Value: $12-$21

Campbell, Mary Mason

1968
New England Butt'ry Shelf Cookboook, The
Campbell, Mary Mason
The World Publishing Co.
Hardcover
192 pages
Illustrations by Tasha Tudor
Value: $37-$66

1971
Betty Crocker's Kitchen Gardens
Campbell, Mary Mason
Universal
Hardcover
170 pages
Illustrations by Tasha Tudor
Value: $23-$41

Carney, Cleve

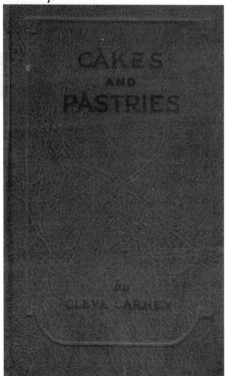

*Inside Page
Sample*

1923
Cakes And Pastries
Carney, Cleve
Calumet
Hardcover
58 pages
270 pastry recipes for professional bakers. Recipes are for large quantities. Exceptional color plates. Additional pages for recording recipes
Value: $88-$156

Child, Julia

Julia Child was nothing short of a culinary phenomenon. Credited far more frequently than her rightful predecessors as the mother of French cuisine in America, the oddly charismatic, infinitely likable Julia charmed members of the culinary elite and common housewives with equal success to become one of the most decorated and beloved food influences the world has ever known. As a woman who took up formal cooking late in life, almost solely to seduce her future husband's affection, this was no small accomplishment.

Julia's first book, *Mastering the Art of French Cooking* (1961), with Simone Beck and Louisette Bertholle, was a culinary landmark that almost didn't make it onto shelves. Beginning tentatively in 1953, Child and her associates scoured the food industry relentlessly for the authoritative recipes, techniques, tips and background that would make it the definitive guide to French cookery for cooks of all levels.

Julia was proactive in finding stateside ingredients to supplement or replace those that could, at that time, only be found in France, ensuring the authenticity of each finished dish the book would produce. Despite this diligent work, publisher Houghton Mifflin rejected the manuscript in 1959. Thankfully, through the efforts of publisher Alfred Knopf and editor Judith Jones, Knopf released *Mastering* in 1961, setting a new standard for cookbooks and stateside cooking simultaneously.

Profoundly successful for its depth, masterful command of cookery and well-plotted recipes, *Mastering* continues to impress, recently inspiring a woman to make every recipe and blog about it.

1961-1966
Mastering The Art Of French Cooking Volume One
Child, Julia; Beck, Simone; Bertholle, Louisette
Alfred A. Knopf
Hardcover
684 pages
Early printings do not indicate volume number. Book club reprints are slightly smaller, but still high quality printings.
Illustrations by Sidonie Coryn. Color jacket illustration by Gigot Rôti.
Book and jacket design by Warren Chappell
Value: $35-$62

Hardcover

1968-1970s
French Chef Cookbook, The
Child, Julia
Alfred A. Knopf
Hardcover
440 pages
Available in hardcover or paperback
Many black-and-white photos of Julia Child at work
Value: $9-$16

1970
Mastering The Art Of French Cooking Volume Two
Child, Julia; Beck, Simone
Alfred A. Knopf
Hardcover
555 pages plus index
Original editions measure 7.5" x 10.25". Book club reprints are slightly smaller. Both editions are high-quality printings and desirable. Volume II is a bit harder to find.
Value: $49-$87

Christensen, Lillian Langseth

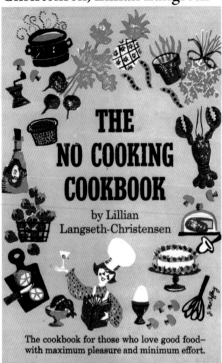

1962
No Cooking Cookbook, The
Christensen, Lillian Langseth
Coward-McCann
Hardcover
255 pages
Value: $15-$35

Church, Ruth Ellen

Food editor for the *Chicago Times* and creator of the popular "Mary Meade" newspaper column, along with many influential columnists, editors and cooks, Ruth Ellen Church lent her considerable expertise as a Pillsbury Grand National Bake-off judge.

1950
Mary Meade Recipes
Church, Ruth Ellen
Chicago Tribune
Stapled booklet
32 pages
Five years of $100 recipes from *Chicago Tribune* "Mary Meade" column. Recipes are attributed to contributors.
Value: $25-$44

Claiborne, Craig

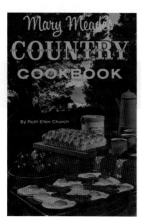

1964
Mary Meade's Country Cookbook
Church, Ruth Ellen
Rand McNally
Hardcover
376 pages
Recipes from the *Chicago Tribune* "Mary Meade" column,
as well as Ruth Ellen Church favorites
Value: $8-$14

1961
New York Times Cook Book, The
Claiborne, Craig
Harper and Row
Hardcover
717 pages
Value: $15-$27

Claire, Mabel

1966
New York Times Menu Cook Book, The
Claiborne, Craig
Harper & Row
Hardcover
729 pages
Companion to *The New York Times Cook Book*
Value: $10-$18

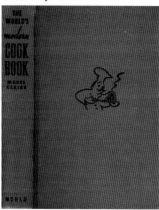

1941
World's Modern Cook Book For The Busy Woman, The
Claire, Mabel
World Publishing
Hardcover
312 pages
Value: $13-$23

Collins, Mary

1964
McCormick Spices Of The World Cookbook, The
Collins, Mary
McGraw-Hill
Hardcover binder
330 pages
2nd Edition. Hard-to-find yellow decorated binder
Value: $53-$94

1969
Spices Of The World By McCormick
Collins, Mary
Penquin for McCormick
Paperback
495 pages
Value: $6-$11

Cooke, Maud

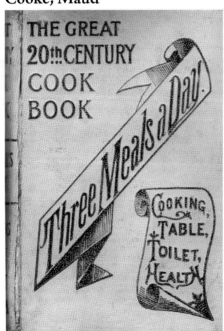

1897
Three Meals A Day: The Great 20th Century Cook Book
Cooke, Maud
Hardcover
A thick and thorough guide with hundreds of recipes, as well as formulas for medicines, flavoring extracts, household chemicals, powders, creams, lipstick and perfumes. A few black-and-white engravings. Frontispiece shows a drawing of the San Francisco Call Building by Claus Spreckels.
Value: $85-$135

Corbitt, Helen

Stanley Marcus, the former president of luxury retail behemoth Neiman Marcus, once called her "the Balenciaga of food." And indeed, for over 20 years Helen Corbitt— author, columnist, food consultant and award-winning cook—was the queen of American cuisine.

A New Yorker by birth, Helen began her food career as a dietitian for Cornell Medical Center. She later relocated to Texas, were she spent almost 40 years catering to (and for) the southern elite with her upscale versions of home style cookery. In 1955, after legendarily turning down President Lyndon Johnson's request that she oversee the White House dining room, Helen finally agreed to Stanley Marcus's plea that she take over food services at his flagship store in Dallas.

Under her control, Neiman Marcus' Zodiac Room became the Mecca of gourmet cuisine in Texas, serving the most sophisticated clientele in the country. Her first book, *Helen Corbitt's Cookbook*, was released in 1957, and was met with critical and commercial enthusiasm. She later went on to win The Golden Plate Award, one of the most coveted awards in the food industry.

1957
Helen Corbitt's Cookbook
Corbitt, Helen
Riverside Press
Hardcover
Famous for the creation of superb recipes for the Zodiac Room of Neiman-Marcus in Dallas. Charming vintage illustrations
Value: $16-$28

1962
Helen Corbitt's Potluck
Corbitt, Helen
Houghton Mifflin
Hardcover
181 pages
Value: $12-$21

1967
Helen Corbitt Cooks For Looks
Houghton Mifflin
Hardcover
115 pages
Value: $10-$18

1974
Helen Corbitt Cooks For Company
Corbitt, Helen
Houghton Mifflin
Hardcover
434 pages
Value: $12-$22

Corson, Juliet

Notable 19th-century food expert and teacher, Juliet Corson was no stranger to poverty or illness. On her own by age 18 after family troubles, the young Juliet began her career as a poorly paid librarian and freelance writer in New York City. Even as success began to find her in the 1870s, she favored services for the poor and ailing, eventually dedicating herself to helping those less fortunate through cooking, nutrition and home economics.

By 1876 Juliet had found a career as a cooking teacher and writer and opened her New York Cooking School, ensuring education that women of all means, rich or poor, could afford by offering tuition on a sliding scale.

Her first three books, including *Fifteen-Cent Dinners for Families of Six* (1877), dealt with cooking on a budget, a theme that carried into (but did not define) her masterwork, *Miss Corson's Practical American Cookery* (1885).

Her friendship with U.S. Commissioner of Education John Eaton led, in part, to the creation of the latter book. His resources at the Bureau of Education gave her access to thousands of recipes and food tips from the country, allowing her to compile a classic guide to regional American cookery.

Despite the success of this and several other books, including her nutrition-based *Manual of Cookery for the Sick* (1892), Juliet found herself ailing and nearly penniless at the end of her life. An impassioned plea was made to her fans for financial assistance, generating a heartfelt response from many donors. Shortly before her death at age 56, the *New York Times* printed a list of donors and their contributions.

Many of Juliet Corson's cookbooks have been recently reproduced. While the value of these reprints to the collector is negligible, they can serve as placeholders until an original copy can be located or afforded.

Home Queen Cook Book, The

Author not noted

M. A. Donohue
Hardcover
608 pages
Subtitled *Two Thousand Valuable Recipes on Cookery and Household Economy, Table Etiquette, Toilet Etc.* Contributions came from over 200 "World's Fair Lady Managers, Wives of Governors, and other Ladies of Position and Influence." Most recipes include a reproduced signature. The book was published in time for the 1893 Chicago World's Fair. A short biography of Juliet Corson is included as an introduction to her position as the director of the exhibit of cooking schools at the Exposition.

The editor or author of this cookbook is not noted, and Julia's contribution is unclear, but the original printing (1893) is listed in Bitting (see sidebar) as James Edson White and Mrs. M. L. Wanless [Anon.]

Value: $102-$181

Crocker, Betty

The ubiquitous Miss Crocker, arguably the most famous American culinary icon, was actually invented in 1921 when a General Mills ad in the *Saturday Evening Post* elicited over 30,000 responses requesting recipes and asking for baking help. Who was the perfect person to answer all these letters? A homey sounding first name was added to the last name of company director, William Crocker, and Betty was born, a bouncing 30-something homemaker, filled with good cheer and cooking savvy. An authoritative yet friendly signature for signing the letters was chosen from employee handwriting samples via a company contest.

Morphing in her image portraits from a grey-haired baking expert to a contemporary cookery professional, Betty has sold over 60 million books since her full-length debut of the 1950s *Betty Crocker's Picture Cook Book*. The book set the standard for all of Betty's (and many other authors') future works, which were designed to make cooking easy, accessible, fun and unfussy, as she reliably remains today.

Betty Crocker's contributions to American cooking are so prolific and iconic, a recent "biography" of Betty documents her success.

Further Reading: *Finding Betty Crocker*, Susan Marks.

See also Recipe Booklets: Crocker, Betty and General Mills.

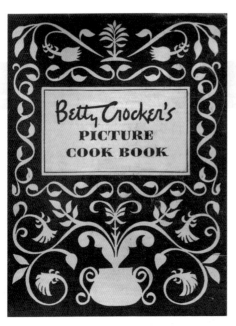

1950
Betty Crocker's Picture Cook Book
Crocker, Betty
General Mills
Hardcover
462 pages
This first edition is available in hardcover and binder configurations. It was recently reprinted in a facsimile edition with plastic cover. Original editions have cloth covers.
Value: $34-$61

1954
Betty Crocker's Good And Easy Cook Book
Crocker, Betty
Simon and Schuster
Hardcover
256 pages
Appealingly small, spiral-bound cookbook with "1,000 time-saving, table-tempting recipes and hints for busy modern homemakers." Illustrated with spot illustrations and color photos
Value: $12-$22

1956
Betty Crocker's Picture Cook Book
Crocker, Betty
McGraw Hill
Hardcover
472 pages
Revised and enlarged 2nd edition. Same contents as gray cover. Available in hardcover or binder
Value: $70-$124

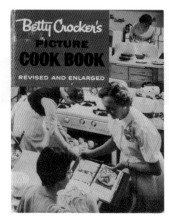

1956
Betty Crocker's Picture Cook Book
Crocker, Betty
McGraw Hill
Hardcover binder
472 pages
Revised and enlarged 2nd edition. Gray cover with red title block. Available as binder or hardcover. Same contents as brown pictorial cover shown above
Value: $39-$69

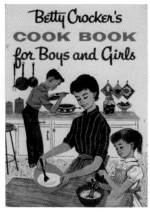

1957
Betty Crocker's Cook Book For Boys And Girls
Crocker, Betty
Simon & Schuster
Hardcover, wire bound
191 pages
Illustrated by Gloria Kamen
Value: $23-$41

1958
Betty Crocker's Dinner For Two Cook Book
Crocker, Betty
Golden Press
Hardcover, wire bound
207 pages
Illustrations by Charles Harper
Value: $16-$28

1959
Betty Crocker's Guide To Easy Entertaining
Crocker, Betty
Golden Press
Hardcover, wire bound
176 pages
Value: $7-$12

1961
Betty Crocker's Outdoor Cook Book
Crocker, Betty
Golden Press
Hardcover, wire bound
176 pages
Illustrations by Tom Funk
Value: $10-$18

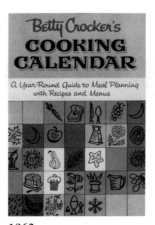

1962
Betty Crocker's Cooking Calendar
Crocker, Betty
Golden Press
Hardcover, wire bound
176 pages
Value: $4-$7

1961-1968
Betty Crocker's New Picture Cook Book
Crocker , Betty
McGraw-Hill
Hardcover binder
454 pages
Available in hardcover or binder edition. Binders command slightly higher prices.
Value: $90-$161

1962
Betty Crocker's New Good And Easy Cookbook
Crocker, Betty
Golden Press
Hardcover, wire bound
192 pages
Illustrations by Rudi Trautmann
Value: $9-$16

1963
Betty Crocker's Cooky Book
Crocker, Betty
Golden Press
Hardcover, wire bound
1963
Illustrations by Eric Mulvany
Value: $22-$39

1964
Betty Crocker's Parties For Children
Freeman, Lois M.
Golden Press
Hardcover, wire bound
166 pages plus index
Illustrated by Judy and Barry Martin
Value: $16-$28

1964
Bisquick Cookbook, The
Crocker, Betty
General Mills
Hardcover, wire bound
112 pages
Illustrations by Roger Bradfield. Look for one that has the original bookmark intact.
Value: $6-$10

1964
Betty Crocker's New Dinner For Two Cookbook
Crocker, Betty
Golden Press
Hardcover, wire bound
156 pages
Illustrated by Margaret Fleming and Jean Simpson
Value: $16-$29

1965
Betty Crocker's Dinner In A Dish Cookbook
Crocker, Betty
Golden Press
Hardcover, wire bound
152 pages plus index
Value: $10-$18

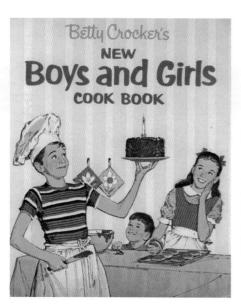

1965
Betty Crocker's New Boys And Girls Cook Book
Crocker, Betty
Golden Press
Hardcover, wire bound
156 pages
Illustrations by Gloria Kamen. Color and black-and-white photos and illustrations
Value: $25-$44

1966
Betty Crocker's Cake And Frosting Mix Cookbook
Crocker, Betty
Golden Press
Hardcover, wire bound
144 pages
Value: $18-$31

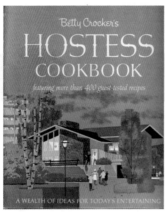

1967
Betty Crocker's Hostess Cookbook
Crocker, Betty
Golden Press
Hardcover, wire bound
168 pages
Illustrations by Deirdre Stanforth
Value: $9-$16

1967
So Quick With New Bisquick
Crocker, Betty
General Mills
Hardcover, wire bound
120 pages
Look for one that still has the bookmark page attached.
Color and black-and-white photos and illustrations
Value: $10-$18

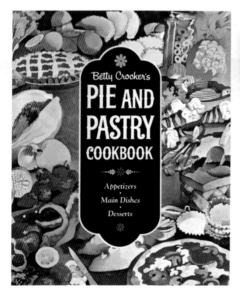

COLLECTING TIP:
Hold onto all original promotional extras found in vintage cookbooks. Things like bookmarks, coupons, special offers, tip-ins and flutter-outs add to the character and value of the book.

1968
Betty Crocker's Pie And Pastry Cookbook
Crocker, Betty
Golden Press
Hardcover, wire bound
160 pages
Illustrations by Bill Goldsmith
Value: $9-$16

1969
Betty Crocker's Cookbook
Crocker, Betty
Golden Press
Hardcover or binder
480 pages
Also known as the "pie" cover as a reference to the graphic shape
Value: $63-$112

1969-1970s
Betty Crocker's Cookbook
Crocker, Betty
Bantam
Paperback
796 pages
Paperback version of the 1969 orange "pie" cover. Originally part of a small slip-covered set that included the *Good and Easy Cookbook, Dinner for Two Cookbook, Dinner Parties* and *Desserts Cookbook.*
Value: $13-$23

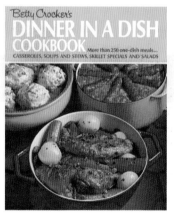

1970
Betty Crocker's Dinner In A Dish Cookbook
Crocker, Betty
Golden Press
Hardcover, wire bound
152 pages plus index
Value: $11-$19

Dahnke, Marye

Opposite the fictional company food experts of the day was Marye Dahnke, a real person, savvy businesswoman and Kraft home economist from 1920 through the '30s. Her 1930s recipe booklet *Favorite Recipes from Marye Dahnke's File* includes a recipe for an iconic American food—Kraft Macaroni and Cheese.

Also look for 1960: *Marye Dahnke's Salad Book.*

See also: Recipe Booklets, Kraft.

Day, Avanelle

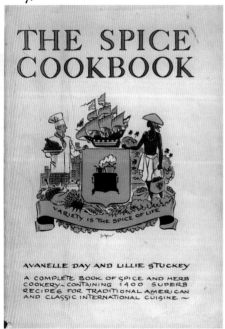

1964
Spice Cookbook, The
Day, Avanelle and Stuckey, Lillie
David White Co.
Hardcover
624 pages
Illustrated by Jo Spier. Includes history of the spice trade, descriptions of each spice and 1,400 recipes
Value: $11-$19

De Proft, Melanie

Sample Booklet

1954-1960
Cooking Magic Or Fabulous Foods Binder Set

De Proft, Melanie (editor)
Culinary Arts
Hardcover binder plus 24 booklets
Complete set of 24 booklets in two, red-and-white, 3"-thick, binders. The name on the binders alternated between *Cooking Magic, Fabulous Foods* and *Cooking Magic Fabulous Foods*. No matter the name, the contents are the same. Binders must be complete and in excellent condition to command the following prices.
Individual booklet values: French, Italian, and Creole—$15-20. Others $3-$10
Value: $137-$244

Booklet List
101. *Quick Dishes*
102. *The Casserole Cookbook*
103. *The French Cookbook*
104. *The Chocolate Cookbook*
106. *The Italian Cookbook*
107. *Breakfast, Brunch and Morning Coffee*
108. *The Ground Meat Cookbook*
109. *Elegant Desserts*
110. *The Creole Cookbook*
111. *Dishes Children Love*
112. *The Gourmet Foods Cookbook*
113. *The Scandinavian Cookbook*
114. *The Hungarian Cookbook*
115. *Entertaining Six or Eight*
116. *The Cheese Cookbook*
117. *Cooling Dishes for Hot Weather*
118. *The New England Cookbook*
119. *Sunday Night Suppers*
120. *The German and Viennese Cookbook*
121. *Cooking with Sour Cream and Buttermilk*
122. *The Southern and Southwestern Cookbook*
123. *Fabulous Low-Calorie Recipes*
124. *The Holiday Cookbook*

1956
American Peoples Cookbook, The
De Proft, Melanie (editor)
Spencer Press
Hardcover
600 pages
Illustrations by Kay Lovelace. Recipes from a contest created by the Culinary Arts Institute. Recipes are attributed to contributors.
Value: $31-$56

1959
My Favorite Recipes
De Proft, Melanie
Spencer Press
Hardcover
320 pages
Illustrations by Kay Lovelace
Value: $10-$18

1961
Woman's World Cook Book
De Proft, Melanie
Culinary Arts
Hardcover
512 pages
Partially based on the *American Woman's Cook Book*, edited by Ruth Berolzheimer
Black-and-white photos
Value: $18-$31

DeBoth, Jessie Marie

A vibrant and charismatic American girl hailing from Appleton, Wis., Jessie DeBoth was a domestic queen bee long before the era of the "how to" TV show. A food writer, home economics expert and author, Jessie wowed audiences in the 1930s during public appearances and demonstrations of cooking techniques and housekeeping hints.

An imposing 6 feet tall, she was a natural born performer who favored giveaways, sing-alongs and audience participation over stuffy lectures, and was known for giving away every meal she prepared onstage.

Jessie's cheery and offbeat style attracted crowds of thousands, and most adoring homemakers waited in line for hours for the opportunity to attend one of her speeches.

She had a popular newspaper column, "Jessie's Notebook," attached to her name, which included endorsements of items like Post Wheat Meal and Sunkist Frozen Lemon Juice. Her cookbooks, including *Modernistic Recipe Menu Book* (1929), the *Fashion Book of Recipes* (1934) and the *Jessie Marie DeBoth Cook Book* (1940) were celebrated for their simple, user-friendly recipes and her attention to both budget and detail.

(*Note:* Her name is alternately spelled with and without the space between syllables as DeBoth and De Both.)

1939
Modern Guide To Better Meals
DeBoth, Jessie Marie
Publisher not noted
Hardcover
374 pages
With calendar of dinners, and abstinence and fast schedules for different faiths
Value: $10-$18

1940
Jessie Marie Deboth's Cook Book
DeBoth, Jessie Marie
Whitman Publishing
Hardcover, wire bound
192 pages
Value: $7-$13

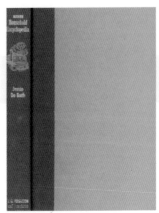

1942
Jessie De Both's Cut Dollars From Your Food Bill Cook Book
DeBoth, Jesse Marie
Consolidated Book Publishers Inc.
Hardcover
374 pages
With calendar of dinners and abstinence schedules.
Formerly published as *Modern Guide to Better Meals*
Value: $28-$50

1946, 1956
Modern Household Encyclopedia
DeBoth, Jessie Marie
Ferguson
Hardcover
316 pages
200 illustrations by Frances Drayton
Value: $6-$10

DeGouy, Louis

A student of the great Auguste Escoffier, Louis DeGouy was a chef's chef. No pretty boy television personality, Louis was a second-generation chef who spent his career cooking in very real and respectable restaurants, most notably as executive chef at the Waldorf-Astoria Hotel (itself once an epicenter of food credited with the Waldorf salad and the rise of Russian dressing, though neither of these contributions was made during his tenure).

Later in his career, Louis began producing a range of cookbooks, all of which were lauded for their charming narrative, detailed explanations and simple, no-nonsense approach to food and cookery. Never one to put technical jargon before loving advice, Louis was a chef who was relatable to even the novice housewife. "Eggs are like some people," he wrote in *The Gold Cook Book* ."Rush them and they get tough. Cook eggs slowly."

Additional Titles:

1937: *Derrydale Fish*
1937: *Derrydale Game*
1939: *The Chef's Cook Book*
1949: *The Pie Book*
1949: *The Soup Book*

1950: *The Salad Book*
1951: *Cocktail Hour*
1951: *The Burger Book*
1944: *The Bread Tray*
1940: *Soda Fountain Drinks*

(Note: His name is alternately spelled with and without the space between syllables as DeGouy and De Gouy.)

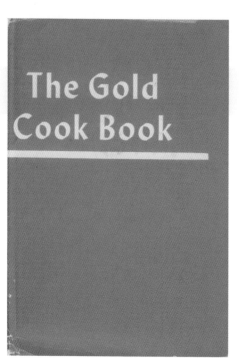

1947-1960s
Gold Cook Book, The
DeGouy, Louis
Chilton
Hardcover
1,256 pages
Reprinted many times with different covers. Shown is the 1960s book club edition with a white cover and gold dust jacket.
Value: $39-$69

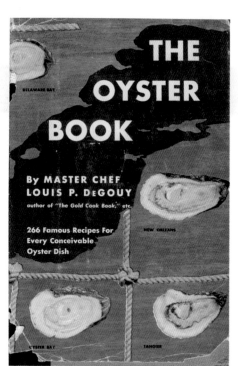

1951
Oyster Book, The
DeGouy, Louis
Greenburg
Hardcover
175 pages
Value: $27-$48

Diat, Louis

Inspired by his mother's breakfast soup and named after the famous French Vichy spa near his native Bourbonnais home, Vichyssoise soup was created by this revolutionary French American chef. A young and inspired chef for the Ritz Carlton in New York from the early 1900s through the '50s, Diat took a scientific approach to cooking, experimenting in his kitchen laboratory with foods from around the world.

His first cookbook, *Sauces, French and Famous* is a work that is still considered a standard on the subject. He later drew on his French roots for his more personal cookbook *French Cooking for the Home* inspired by his mother's cooking. The Bourbonnais recipes are lavish with milk, cream, butter, cheese, eggs and wine, and complemented by lively stories of typical French cookery.

Dietz, F. Meredith

1956
French Cooking For The Home
Diat, Louis
Hammond and Hammond
Hardcover
Value: $13-$24

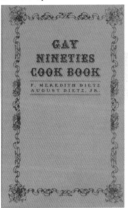

1945
Gay Nineties Cook Book
Dietz, F. Meredith and Dietz, August Jr.
Dietz
Hardcover
318 pages
Recipes, etiquette, tonics and toasts gleaned from "receipt books" published between 1892 and 1895
Value: $15-$28

Dixon, Martha

Popular hostess of the 1960s WJIM-TV *Copper Kettle Show* in Lansing, Mich. Win Schuler, creator of the award-winning Midwest restaurant bearing his name called Dixon's book a "masterpiece."

Doherty, James J.

1963
Martha Dixon's Copper Kettle Cook Book
Dixon, Martha
Wm. B. Eerdmans Publishing
Hardcover
480 pages
Illustrations by Ilse Eerdmans Weidenaar. Book design and calligraphy by Cornelius Lambregetse
Value: $34-$61

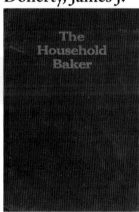

1907
Household Baker, The
Doherty, James J.
Sprecher-Chaplin
Hardcover
190 pages
"A practical treatise on the art of bread and pastry baking as applied to households." Scarce, small baking book by accomplished hotel and bakery chef James Doherty
Value: $46-$81

Ellison, Virginia H.

THE POOH
COOK BOOK

Inspired by WINNIE-THE-POOH and
THE HOUSE AT POOH CORNER by A. A. Milne

By Virginia H. Ellison

Illustrated by Ernest H. Shepard

COLLECTING TIP

Easy, tasty fun-food recipes written and designed to capture kids' interest, cookbooks for children comprise a collectible category in and of themselves.

1969-1975
Pooh Cook Book, The
Ellison, Virginia H.
Dutton
Hardcover
120 pages
Charming little cookbook with many "pooh-isms." Every recipe is made with honey. Illustrated by Ernest H. Shepard
Recipes include: Poohanopiglet Pancakes, Popovers for Piglet, Fairy Toast and Hipy Papy Bthuthdth Thuthda Bthuthdy Cake.
Value: $28-$49

Engle, Fannie

1946
Fannie Engle's Cook Book
Engle, Fannie
Duell, Sloan and Pearce
Hardcover
186 pages
Value: $12-$21

1954
Jewish Festival Cookbook, The
Engle, Fannie and Blair, Gertrude
Paperback Library
Paperback
216 pages
Value: $11-$19

Ervin, Janet Halliday

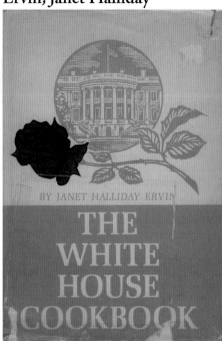

1964
White House Cookbook, The
Ervin, Janet Halliday
Follett Publishing
Hardcover
510 pages
Includes a brief history of the original 1887 *White House Cook Book*. Retains many recipes from the original edition, adding a number of recipes from Frances Cleveland's era that were not found in the first edition, as well as recipes from the 14 first ladies.
Black-and-white photos and drawings
Value: $14-$24

Esquire

1949
Esquire's Handbook For Hosts
Editors of *Esquire Magazine*
Grosset & Dunlap
Hardcover
288 pages
Highly illustrated bachelor guide to cocktails, food and etiquette. Design and Typography by A. P. Tedesco. Witty and stylish
Value: $41-$74

Farm Journal

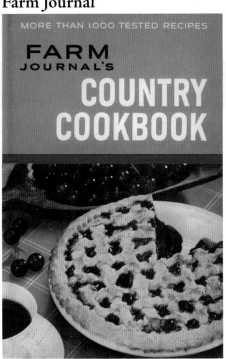

1959

Farm Journal's Country Cookbook

Nichols, Nell B. (editor)
Doubleday
Hardcover
Printed with several distinct covers. Showing "Deluxe Edition"
Value: $41-$73

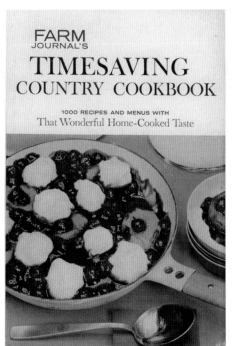

1961

Farm Journal's Timesaving Country Cookbook

Editors of *Farm Journal*
Farm Journal
Hardcover
254 pages
Value: $11-$19

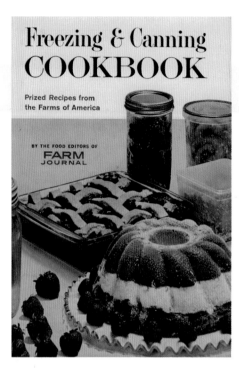

1964
Farm Journal Freezing And Canning Cookbook
Nichols, Nell B. (editor)
Farm Journal
Hardcover
315 pages
Value: $20-$36

1966
Let's Start To Cook
Nichols, Nell B. (editor)
Doubleday & Co.
Hardcover
254 pages
Value: $13-$23

1969
Homemade Bread
Nichols, Nell B. (editor)
Farm Journal
Hardcover
152 pages
Value: $17-$31

1970
Homemade Candy
Farm Journal
Doubleday
Hardcover
224 pages
More than 250 candy recipes including 50 for fudge alone
Value: $16-$28

1971
Farm Journal Homemade Cookies
Nichols, Nell B. (editor)
Doubleday & Co.
Hardcover
320 pages
Value: $21-$37

Farmer, Fannie Merritt

One of the most influential cookbook authors and domestic science experts to emerge from New England during the end of the 1800s, Fannie Farmer was best known for her involvement with The Boston Cooking School. A bright girl, Fannie had to shelve plans to attend college when illness forced her out of school. To cope, she made herself useful around the home, helping to keep house and learning her way around the kitchen (her father, a professor, would bring her recipes from his travels). Her domestic skill eventually led her to the Boston Cooking School, where she enrolled in 1888.

After graduating Fannie joined the faculty, serving as principal from 1893-1902. It was during this time that she, building upon the foundation that Mrs. Mary Lincoln had laid, penned her *Boston Cooking School Cookbook* (1896). The book, oft credited as one of the first to standardize recipe measurements and discuss troubleshooting, was a smash success. Her uniform measures made recipe results more reliable, and the shrewd Fannie had included trend-driven recipes that attracted upper-class hostesses to its pages.

The book enjoyed decades of printings with roughly 3 million copies sold by the mid-1950s, and became the gold standard for cookbooks to follow. After Fannie's death in 1915, the book's legacy was handed down to her niece, who continued to edit and revise it for modern kitchens. In 1979, a twelfth edition was released by James Beard protégé Marion Cunningham, and it sold 400,000 copies that year alone. During her life, Fannie opened Miss Farmer's School of Cookery and wrote several other cookery books, however none of her subsequent titles had the lingering influence of *The Boston Cooking School Cook Book*.

1896, 1973
Original Boston Cooking School Cook Book 1896, The
Farmer, Fannie Merritt
Weathervane Books
Hardcover
568 pages plus ads
1st edition, a facsimile reprint of the first edition of the *Boston Cooking-School Cook Book*. Eighteen pages of period advertisements at back of book
Value: $16-$28

1904
Boston Cooking-School Cook
Farmer, Fannie Merritt
Little, Brown and Co.
Hardcover
Unclear if this is considered the 2nd edition or a modified first edition. Revised with an appendix of 300 recipes and an addendum of 60 recipes.
666 pages plus 20 pages of advertising
Value: $88-$156

1905, 1970
What To Have For Dinner
Farmer, Fannie Merritt
Dodge
Hardcover
271 pages
Value: $27-$48

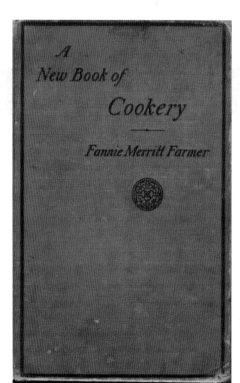

1912
New Book Of Cookery, A
Farmer, Fannie Merritt
Little, Brown & Co.
Hardcover
Considered a sequel and companion to *The Boston Cooking-School Cook Book* and later compiled into books of that title
Over 800 recipes, six color plates and 200 half-tone illustrations
440 pages plus approximately 24 pages of ads
Value: $46-$81

1918-1922
Boston Cooking-School Cook Book, The
Farmer, Fannie Merritt
Little, Brown and Co.
Hardcover
656 pages
3rd edition. The 1918 Revised Edition of the Fannie Farmer classic with additional chapters on the cold pack method of canning, on the drying of fruits and vegetables, and on food values
Edited by Mary Farmer
Only the 1918 printing includes wartime recipe supplement
122 half-tone illustrations
Value: $53-$94

1923-1929
Boston Cooking-School Cook Book, The
Perkins, Cora (editor)
Little, Brown, & Co.
Hardcover
808 pages plus ads
4th edition. 1923 edition is a major revision, incorporating Miss Farmer's 1912 *A New Book of Cookery*. Cover colors for these years vary slightly.
122 half-tone illustrations
Approx. 40 additional pages of ads at back of book
Value: $39-$69

1930-1935
Boston Cooking-School Cook Book, The
Perkins, Wilma Lord (editor)
Little, Brown, & Co.
Hardcover
5th Edition
831 pages with approximately 25-30 additional pages of advertisements
1933 printing includes an ad for Miss Farmer's School of Cookery. Cover colors vary slightly but recipe contents are identical for any printing of this edition.
Value: $37-$66

1936-1939
Boston Cooking-School Cook Book, The
Perkins, Wilma Lord (editor)
Little, Brown and Co.
Hardcover
838 pages plus ads
6th edition. Note that the dust jacket for this edition erroneously refers to this printing as the Fifth Edition, but the title page notes that it is the 6th edition.
Value: $39-$69

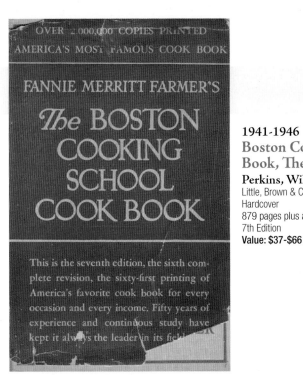

1941-1946
Boston Cooking-School Cook Book, The
Perkins, Wilma Lord (editor)
Little, Brown & Co.
Hardcover
879 pages plus ads
7th Edition
Value: $37-$66

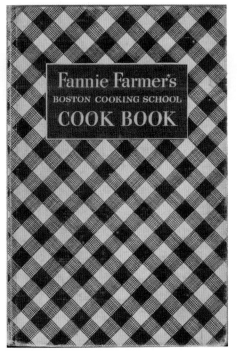

1946-1950
Fannie Farmer's Boston Cooking School Cook Book
Perkins, Wilma Lord (editor)
Little, Brown
Hardcover
879 pages
8th Edition. Black-and-white illustrations
Value: $34-$61

1951-1954
New Fannie Farmer Boston Cooking-School Cook Book, The
Perkins, Wilma Lord (editor)
Little, Brown and Co.
Hardcover
878 pages
9th Edition. Drawings by Barbara Corrigan. Color and black-and-white photos and illustrations
Value: $34-$61

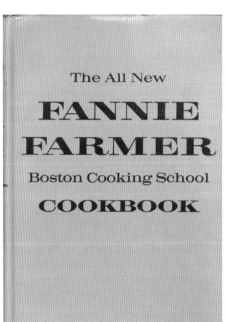

1959
All New Fannie Farmer Boston-Cooking School Cookbook, The
Perkins, Wilma Lord (editor)
Little, Brown and Co.
Hardcover
596-plus pages
10th Edition. First printing of the 1959 edition. 596 pages plus blank pages for notes and recipes. Illustrations by Alison Mason Kingsbury. There are several other printings of the 10th edition, but contents are identical.
Value: $60-$106

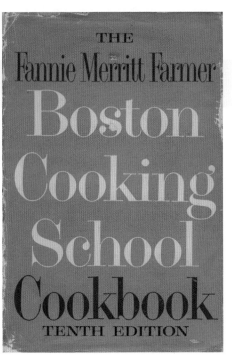

1959-1963
Fannie Merritt Farmer Boston Cooking School Cookbook, The
Perkins, Wilma Lord (editor)
Boston, Little, Brown and Co.
Hardcover
596 pages
10th Edition. Illustrations by Allison Mason Kingsbury. Tan linen cover with red or brown titles. Includes a complete listing of all editions through the 10th
Value: $39-$69

1965-1970s
All New Fannie Farmer Boston Cooking School Cookbook, The
Perkins, Wilma Lord (editor)
Bantam
Paperback
648 pages
10th Edition. Same contents as earlier printings of the 10th edition. Available with several slightly different cover designs, but contents identical.
Value: $21-$38

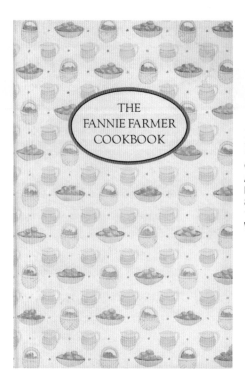

1979-1980s
Fannie Farmer Cookbook, The
Cunningham, Marion (editor)
Alfred A. Knopf
Hardcover
811 pages
12th Edition
Value: $11-$19

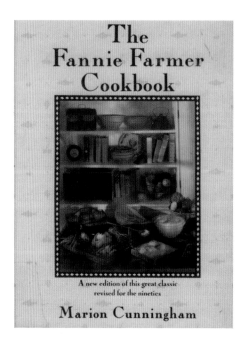

1990
Fannie Farmer Cookbook, The
Cunningham, Marion (editor)
Knopf
Hardcover
874 pages
13th Edition
Value: $17-$31

Fisher, Marian Cole

Early 20th-century lecturer and promoter of the science of the kitchen and cookery, Marian Cole Fisher (Mrs. W. A. Wittbecker) was known to nearly every household in the city of St. Paul, Minn., as the writer of the "Kitchen Clinic" newspaper column. Sometimes described as a suffragette, she spoke plainly in a 1911 *Pioneer Press* article, scolding a St. Louis professor for blaming the high cost of living on the homemaker—"If the professor had ever stood in a kitchen over a range or a sink ... he would be in a better position to offer advice."

Her book *Twenty Lessons in Domestic Science* shows design layouts for the efficient kitchen, and she was an early advocate of convenience-style cooking to free women from unending kitchen duties. At the 1924 Dispatch-Pioneer Press Food Show, she demonstrated a special method of eliminating the drudgery of pot washing by cooking an entire meal in separate paper packets.

Local papers announced her suicide in 1929, apparently over a financial scandal involving her daughter and her husband.

Note that her name is alternately spelled with an "o" as "Marion."

See also Recipe Booklets: Calumet.

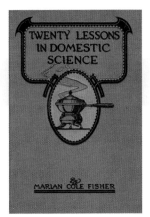

1916
Twenty Lessons In Domestic Science
Fisher, Marian Cole
Calumet
Hardcover
108 pages
Compiled and printed for the Calumet Baking Powder Co. and presented with its compliments
Value: $23-$74

1927
Marian Cole Fisher Handbook Of Cookery
Fisher, Marion Cole
Publisher not noted
Hardcover
814 pages
Cloth green gingham cover with titles adhered as die-cut labels. Local (Minnesota) and national advertisements
Value: $46-$81

Ford Motor Co.

1950
Favorite Recipes From Famous Eating Places
Kennedy, Nancy (editor)
Simon and Schuster
Soft cover, wire bound
252 pages plus map
Value: $20-$36

1954
Ford Treasury Of Favorite Recipes From Famous Eating Places Vol. 2
Kennedy, Nancy (editor)
Ford Motor Co.
Soft cover, wire bound or hardcover
253 pages
Many color illustrations of each restaurant by numerous period artists, including Charles Harper, Allen Reed and Robert Collins. Available in hardcover and soft cover. Hardcover has a different cover and is titled *The Second Ford Treasury of Favorite Recipes from Famous Eating Places.*
2nd in a series
Value: $32-$56

1959
Ford Treasury Of Favorite Recipes From Famous Eating Places
Kennedy, Nancy (editor)
Golden Press
Soft cover, wire bound
252 pages
Volume 3
Value: $23-$41

1964
New Ford Treasury Of Favorite Recipes From Famous Restaurants
Kennedy, Nancy (editor)
Ford Motor
Hardcover
144 pages
Third printing revised
Value: $16-$28

1968

Ford Times Cookbook, The

Kennedy, Nancy (editor)
Simon and Schuster
Hardcover
253 pages
Fifth in a series. Highly illustrated with expert color drawings by some of the best illustrators of the era. Regrettably, unlike earlier issues, the illustrators are not credited.
Value: $25-$44

Frolov, Wanda L.

1947

Katish, Our Russian Cook

Frolov, Wanda L.
Farrar
Hardcover
208 pages
A novel and cookbook follows the daily life of the author's Russian cook. Part fiction, part cookbook
Illustrations by Henry J. Stahlhut. Designed by Stefan Salter
Value: $11-$19

Gaige, Crosby

Also revised the 2nd edition of *André Simon's French Cook Book.*

See also Cookbooks: Simon, André.

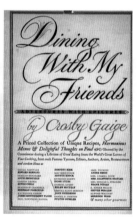

1949

Dining With My Friends

Gaige, Crosby
Crown Publishers
Hardcover
292 pages
Value: $26-$47

General Foods

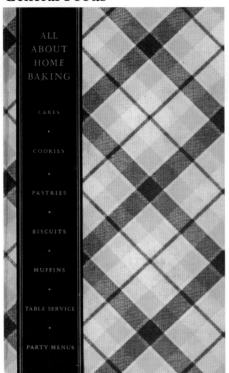

1933-1939
All About Home Baking
General Foods
General Foods
Hardcover
144 pages
Highly illustrated with charming period color illustrations and black-and-white, step-by-step photos. Also available as soft cover
Value: $20-$36

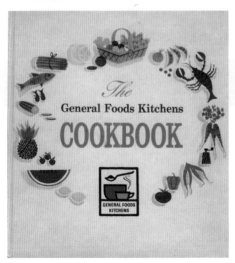

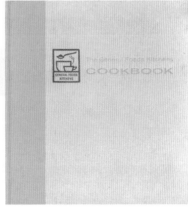

1959
General Foods Kitchens Cookbook, The
The Women of General Foods Kitchens
Random House
Hardcover, also available in soft cover
436 pages
Available in two cover designs, identical contents
Illustrated by Mary Ronin. Photos by George Lazarnick
Value: $13-$23

Gillard, Barbara

1951
Pass Me Another
Gillard, Barbara
The Letter Shop
Soft cover, wire bound
Un-paginated
Die-cut cheese shape design with thick wire binding
Illustrations by Edmund Gross
Value: $25-$44

1952
Pot Luck
Gillard, Barbara
The Letter Shop
Soft cover, thick wire binding
64 pages
Cover and illustrations by Edmund Gross
Value: $23-$42

1953
Clock Wise
Gillard, Barbara
The Letter Shop
Soft cover, wire bound
67 pages
Cover and illustrations by Edmund Gross
Value: $17-$41

Gillette, Fanny Lemira

Gillette published her original *White House Cook Book* in 1887 at the age of 60 years old. She built this encyclopedic cookbook over her 40 years as the mistress of her own household and along with hundreds of practical recipes, it includes gracious sections on making cosmetics and cleaners, childcare and laundry and directions for the multitude of tasks required of the Victorian homemaker, making it a favorite gift for the new bride.

The title of this first edition seems to promise a glimpse into the White House kitchens, but aside from some nice engravings of first ladies it lacks any White House trivia. Subsequent editions were co-authored with Hugo Ziemann, White House steward, and included interesting facts like seating plans and etiquette for state occasions at the White House, engravings showing White House kitchen and dining rooms, and menus served on special occasions.

Additional titles:
1891: *The Household Gem Cyclopædia*
1895: *The Presidential Cook Book*
1897: *Mrs. Gillette's Cook Book*

1894
White House Cook Book, The
Gillette, F. L. Mrs.; Ziemann, Hugo
Werner Co.
Hardcover
570 pages
Frontispiece engraving of Frances Folsom Cleveland. Many additional engravings and drawings throughout
White cover with silver embossed titles
Value: $105-$188

1900
White House Cook Book, The
Gillette, Mrs. F. L.; Ziemann, Hugo
Saalfield Publishing
Hardcover
590 pages
New and enlarged edition
590 pages plus two pages of advertisements for other Saalfield books
Engravings and photos of first ladies, and additional black-and-white illustrations
Value: $53-$94

Given, Meta

Another food and home economics expert credited with the advent of the "mother book," or a guide to all things homemaking, Meta Given started out as a humble farm girl in the Ozark Mountains. Interested in the link between food and health, she studied nutrition and food at the Universities of Missouri, Wisconsin and Chicago.

After completing school, she gained notoriety as a nutrition expert with a keen sensibility, and wrote recipes, newspaper columns and cookbooks aimed at providing nutritionally balanced meals on any budget. Her nationally syndicated column, "Easy Preparation of Good and Nutritious Meals," eventually led to books like *The Modern Family Cook Book* (1942) and *Meta Given's Modern Encyclopedia of Cooking* (1947). The former garnered critical acclaim when it was published—the *Chicago Tribune* called it "something new in cookbooks," citing its nutritionally sound menus and detailed buying guides—and Meta's style went on to set the tone for many cookbooks to come.

She was respected as the go-to girl for easy, balanced recipes executed by homemaking novices and expert cooks alike, and her *Encyclopedia of Cooking* enjoyed over a half dozen printings.

1942
Modern Family Cook Book, The
Given, Meta
J. Ferguson
Hardcover
938 pages
First edition of *The Modern Family Cook Book*, thumb-indexed with red spray decoration on the book fore edges. Highly illustrated with color photos and black-and-white drawings, charts and tables
Value: $46-$81

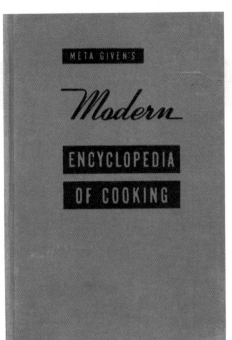

1947-1951

Meta Given's Modern Encyclopedia Of Cooking Set

Given, Meta
J. G. Ferguson and Assoc.
Hardcover
Two-volume set. Black-and-white photos and illustrations
Value: $40-$81

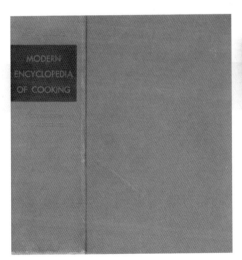

DEFINITION

Thumb-indexed: Small half-moon indentations in the fore edges of a book allowing an easy way to access sections.

1947-1955

Meta Given's Modern Encyclopedia Of Cooking

Given, Meta
J. Ferguson & Assoc.
Hardcover
1,702 pages
This edition combines two volumes into one complete volume.
Value: $56-$99

Dust Jacket

1953, 1958, 1961
Modern Family Cook Book, The
Given, Meta
J. G. Ferguson
Hardcover
632 pages
Showing 1958 book club edition with bean pot endpapers.
Some printings have pink candy endpapers. 1958-1961
printings have an added page for altitude cookery, but
otherwise no difference in contents.
Value: $29-$52

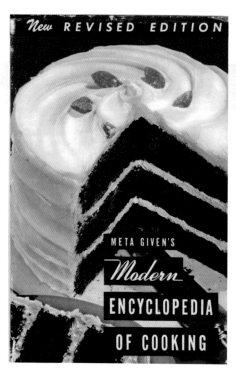

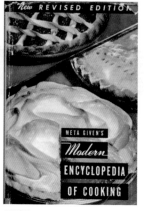

1959
Meta Given's Modern Encyclopedia Of Cooking New Revised Edition Set
Given, Meta
J. G. Ferguson and Assoc.
Hardcover
1,534 pages
Set of two volumes totaling 1,534 pages. Original edition has
photographic endpapers.
Value: $63-$112

Good Housekeeping

Good Housekeeping magazine was founded in 1885, spawned the Good Housekeeping Institute in 1900, and the first *Good Housekeeping Approved Cookbook* in 1903.

Founder Clarke W. Bryan envisioned an institution dedicated to helping women with all facets of homemaking. And, in an era lacking any real control over food safety and purity, the institution was a leader in the fight for The Pure Food and Drug Act of 1906.

By the 1930s, the institute was well established as an authority and a "clearing house of information on questions relating to the keeping and management" of the home. The laboratories tested kitchen equipment used in housekeeping for durability, design and safety.

1920s British versions of the *Good Housekeeping Cookbooks* were printed under the titles *Good Housekeeping Cookery Book* and *Good Housekeeping Menu & Recipe Book*.

COLLECTING TIP

The early *Good Housekeeping* and many other antique cookbooks contain extra "Memoranda" pages scattered throughout to be used for additional recipes. Cookbooks with handwritten recipes command higher prices, so look for copies that have notes and recipes on these pages.

1903
Good Housekeeping Everyday Cook Book
Curtis, Isabel Gordon (editor)
Good Housekeeping
Hardcover
314 pages plus index
The first Good Housekeeping cookbook
Value: $25-$44

1909
Good Housekeeping Woman's Home Cook Book
Curtis, Isabel Gordon (editor)
Reilly & Britton Co.
Hardcover
320 pages
Value: $60-$106

1922-1926

Good Housekeeping's Book Of Menus, Recipes, And Household Discoveries

Good Housekeeping editors
Good Housekeeping
Hardcover
254 pages
Some editions have an intro page with photos of the Good Housekeeping Institute.
Contributors noted by initials and location
Tenth edition, with the 1925 printing billed as "revised," but if there is a difference, it is not easily discernible.
Value: $10-$18

1927

Good Meals And How To Prepare Them

Fisher, Katherine (editor)
Good Housekeeping Institute
Hardcover
256 pages
Tan cover with red embossed checkerboard. Given as a premium to *Good Housekeeping* subscribers
Value: $17-$31

1930

Meals Tested, Tasted, And Approved

Good Housekeeping editors
Good Housekeeping
Hardcover
256 pages
Offered as a premium to *Good Housekeeping Magazine* subscribers
Value: $12-$21

1933-1935

Good Housekeeping Cook Book Recipes And Methods

Good Housekeeping editors
Good Housekeeping
Hardcover
254 pages
Value: $27-$48

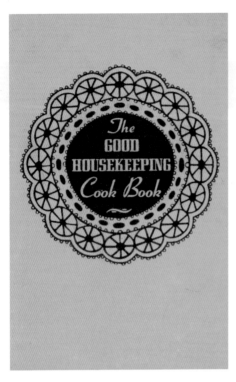

1943
Good Housekeeping Cook Book, The

Marsh, Dorothy B. (editor)
International Readers League or Stamford House
Hardcover
950 pages
This cover is used for two versions. 1943: contains 950 pages plus a 32-page wartime supplement. The Preface to the Third Edition states that the book includes a wartime supplement after page 694. However, the 32-page supplement is actually between pages 582 and 583 and does not affect the pagination of the book.
1944: completely revised edition contains a Preface to the 7th Edition, 981 pages and no wartime supplement.
Value: $31-$66

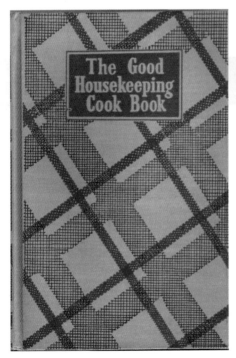

Dust Jacket

1944
Good Housekeeping Cook Book, The

Marsh, Dorothy B. (editor)
Rinehart & Co.
Hardcover
981 pages
Same contents as the second printing of the doily cover.
Value: $54-$96

Dust Jacket

1955
Good Housekeeping Cook Book
Marsh, Dorothy B. (editor)
Hearst
Hardcover
760 pages
Value: $52-$93

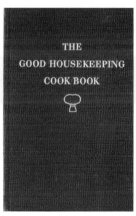

1949
Good Housekeeping Cook Book, The

Marsh, Dorothy B. (editor)
Stamford or Reinhart
Hardcover
1,014 pages
Value: $45-$81

COLLECTING TIP

Wartime editions, whether World War I or World War II, generally command higher prices. Look for books that contain supplemental wartime sections, rationing advice, recipes for egg-less cakes, sugar substitutes and use of less-expensive cuts of meat due to wartime shortages.

Sample Booklet

Booklet List
1. *Appetizer Book*
2. *Book of Cookies*
3. *Cake Book*
4. *Quick 'N' Easy*
5. *Casserole Book*
6. *Book of Salads*
7. *Party Pie Book*
8. *Hamburger & Hot Dog Book*
9. *Meat Cook Book*
10. *Book of Vegetables*
11. *Book of Delectable Desserts*
12. *Egg and Cheese Spaghetti and Rice Dishes*
13. *Breads & Sandwiches*
14. *Company Meals and Buffets*
15. *Fish and Shellfish Book*
16. *Poultry & Game Book*
17. *Ice Creams & Cool Drinks*
18. *Ten P.M. Cook Book*
19. *Around the World Cook Book*
20. *Who's Who Cooks*

1958, 1959
Good Housekeeping's Cook Books (20 Booklets Plus Binder)
Good Housekeeping editors
Good Housekeeping/Consolidated Books
Hardcover binder plus 20 booklets
Twenty separate Good Housekeeping recipe booklets, each
with 68 pages, make up the chapters in this enormous
classic. Each booklet is charming on its own and is notable
for its exceptional period illustrations by various artists.
Spot color drawings, black and white and color photos
Value: $88-$156

Dust Jacket

1963
Good Housekeeping Cookbook, The
Marsh, Dorothy B. (editor)
Harcourt Brace & World
Hardcover
805 pages
Illustrations by Bill Goldsmith
Value: $20-$36

1964
Good Housekeeping International Cookbook, The
Marsh, Dorothy B. (editor)
Good Housekeeping Book Div.
Hardcover
245 pages
Illustrations by Bill Goldsmith
Value: $9-$16

Greenbaum, Florence Kreisler

Dust Jacket

1973
Good Housekeeping Cookbook
Coulson, Zoe (editor)
Good Housekeeping Books
Hardcover
811 pages
Value: $37-$66

1918, 1931, 1940
Jewish Cook Book, The
Greenbaum, Florence Kreisler
Bloch Publishing
Hardcover
438 pages
Reprinted many times. The 1940 edition is shown here, yet earlier editions command higher prices.
Value: $102-$181

Gregory, Annie

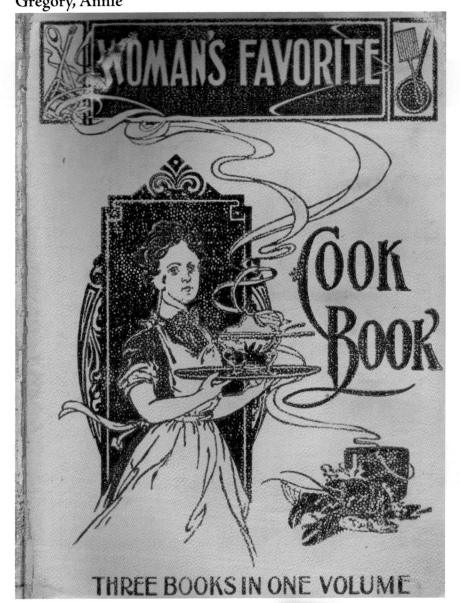

1902
Woman's Favorite Cook Book

Gregory, Annie
Hardcover
578 pages
Embellished with many colored and photo engravings. Written by Annie Gregory "for 10 years chef of the Union League Club, Chicago, now of Grand Pacific Hotel," who was assisted by 1,000 homemakers. Many cosmetic recipes like creams, tooth powder, cure for rough skin, shampoos, recipe "to make a handsome throat," etc. Recipes attributed to contributors
Value: $88-$156

COLLECTING TIP
Books offering homemaking advice including household hints, recipes for cosmetics and formulas for cleaning and healing are popular among many collectors.

Harwood, Jim

1969
Soul Food
Harwood, Jim and Callahan, Ed
Nitty Gritty
Soft cover
210 pages
More than 200 recipes including corn custard, pokeweed, muddy rice and spareribs.
Designed by Reis and Manwaring. Black-and-white illustrations
Value: $11-$19

Herter, George and Herter, Berthe

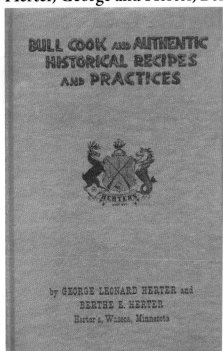

1969, 1970
**Bull Cook And Authentic
Historical Recipes And Practices
Three Volume Set**
Herter, George and Herter, Berthe
Herter's Inc.
Hardcover
Three-volume set
A self-published masterpiece of cooking miscellany, historic recipes and comments on the state of things. Engaging irreverent style with enormous range of recipes and advice from making onion soup to preparing for a cobalt bomb attack. Black-and-white photos
Value: $102-$181

Heseltine, Marjorie

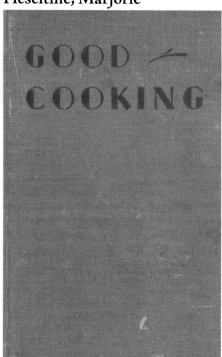

1936
Good Cooking Made Easy And Economical
Heseltine, Marjorie and Dow, Ula
Houghton Mifflin
Hardcover
561 pages
A basic cookbook aimed at the new bride
Black-and-white illustrations of cooking techniques
Shown is the new edition, revised and enlarged to include
chapters on home canning, preserves, jellies and pickles.
Value: $14-$25

1949
Hood Basic Cook Book, The
Heseltine, Marjorie and Dow, Ula
Houghton Mifflin
Hardcover
740 pages plus index
Revised and enlarged edition of *Good Cooking Made Easy
and Economical.*
Includes the story and history of the New Hampshire
Hood Dairy. A variation on the *Basic Cook Book* also by
Heseltine and Dow. This version was produced for the dairy
and includes a 100-plus-page photo supplement with
bibliography.
Black and white photos
Value: $41-$73

1957
New Basic Cook Book, The
Heseltine, Marjorie and Dow, Ula
Riverside Press
Hardcover
718 pages
Value: $46-$81

Dust Jacket

Hiller, Elizabeth O.

A domestic expert, home economics teacher and cookbook author, Elizabeth O. Hiller took the household sciences seriously.

" ... cookery has become an art, a noble Science," she wrote in the preface to her *Practical Cook Book* (1910). A consummate teacher, she taught cooking classes out of a department store in Denver and was the principal of the Chicago Domestic Science School. For those who couldn't come to her, she toured the country lecturing and giving demonstrations.

Her books were lively and comprehensive, and carried *The Practical Cook Book's* enthusiastic self-importance. With her *Fifty-Two Sunday Dinners* (1915), she joined the ranks of Sarah Tyson Rorer, Janet M. Hill and Marion Harland by touting the divinity of Cottolene, a revolutionary "healthy" cooking fat made from cottonseed oil and beef tallow.

Hiller's most interesting and collectible work, however, was a series of calendar cookbooks—365 recipe-dense guides to various food items accented with characteristic art deco and art nouveau illustrations. Acting as both kitchen art and cookbook, they are adorned with thick satin cords for hanging.

Circa 1920
**Calendar Of Sandwiches &
Beverages**
Hiller, Elizabeth O.
P.F. Volland Co.
Soft cover
60 pages
Undated, circa 1920. We know of two available cover designs. Box or slipcase adds value.
Value: $45-$75

Hines, Duncan

Adventures In Good Cooking And The Art Of Carving In The Home
Hines, Duncan
Duncan Hines
Soft cover
Un-paginated
Shown are covers of the 1951, 21st printing, 607 recipes, plus carving and index sections; and the 1955, 26th printing, 713 recipes plus carving and index sections
Other: 1960, 29th printing, 607 recipes plus carving and index sections
Value: $14-$21

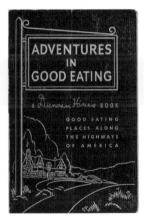

1945
Adventures In Good Eating
Hines, Duncan
Soft cover
283 pages
28th printing shown
Value: $11-$19

1955
Duncan Hines Dessert Book, The
Hines, Duncan
Pocket
Paperback
362 pages
Recipes attributed to contributors, including chefs from around the country
Value: $11-$19

Hollister, Will C.

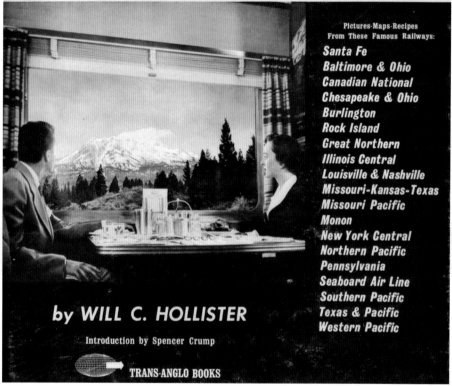

Dinner in the Diner

GREAT RAILROAD RECIPES OF ALL TIME

Pictures-Maps-Recipes
From These Famous Railways:

Santa Fe
Baltimore & Ohio
Canadian National
Chesapeake & Ohio
Burlington
Rock Island
Great Northern
Illinois Central
Louisville & Nashville
Missouri-Kansas-Texas
Missouri Pacific
Monon
New York Central
Northern Pacific
Pennsylvania
Seaboard Air Line
Southern Pacific
Texas & Pacific
Western Pacific

by WILL C. HOLLISTER

Introduction by Spencer Crump

TRANS-ANGLO BOOKS

1965
Dinner In The Diner: Great
Railroad Recipes Of All Time
Hollister, Will C.
Trans-Anglo Books
Hardcover
144 pages
Third revised edition shown
Value: $41-$73

Household Magazine

B eginning in the late 1800s as a general interest publication with a conscious Christian slant, *Household Magazine* became one of many well-known magazines aimed at the American housewife and her family. Featuring articles on cooking, baking, beauty, kitchen décor, romance, entertainment and more, the magazine was an appealing one-stop publication for women's interest material.

Many issues featured fiction writing and essays, but as edited in the late 1920s through the 1950s by Nelson Antrim Crawford, the magazine was rarely listed for its literary relevance and remained primarily a fluffy guide for modern women. Though it encountered one notable scandal in the mid-1880s (the publisher and magazine were accused of lottery fraud and were seized by police in 1884), *Household* was a quirky, squeaky-clean slice of female Americana epitomized by Rockwellian covers featuring dream homes and smiling families.

In 1931, *Household* published its first book, the *Household Searchlight Recipe Book*. A compendium of recipes combined with concise cooking instructions and tips, the book has been in print over 70 years and is still a well-loved companion in many kitchens. It was followed by *Household's Searchlight Homemaking Guide* in 1937, though the latter never gained the notoriety of its older sister. The recently reprinted version does not retain the thumb-tabbed sections.

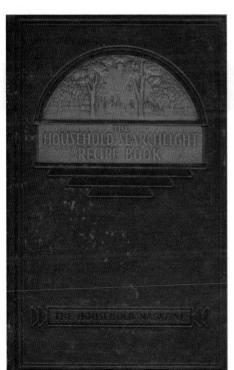

1935-1941
Household Searchlight Recipe Book
Household Magazine, The
Hardcover
289-plus blank pages
1st through 14th editions have identical contents.
Thumb-indexed
Compiled and edited by: Migliario, Ida; Allard, Harriett; Titus, Zorada; and Nunemaker, Irene
Value: $39-$69

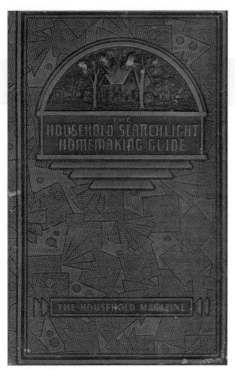

1937
Household Searchlight Homemaking Guide
Household Magazine Staff
Household Magazine
Hardcover
320 pages
Exceptional guide to homemaking circa 1937 with tabbed sections that cover the trousseau, getting married, home decor, laundry, the lawn, household pests, child care and much more. Outstanding embossed art deco cover design
Value: $25-$44

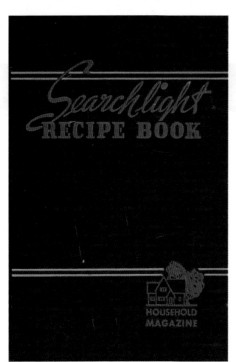

1942-1980s
Searchlight Recipe Book, The
Household Magazine Staff
Household Magazine, The
Hardcover
320 pages
15th through 21st editions have identical contents. Thumb-indexed until the 1980s
Value: $27-$49

Howard, Munroe

75¢ A Paperback Library 📖 Easy-to-Cookbook 64-320

More than 150 recipes designed to please any man

Sex Pots... And Pans

The single girl's guide to hooking her man—through cooking

By Munroe Howard

1970
Sex Pots And Pans
Howard, Munroe
Paperback Library
Paperback
144 pages
150 ways to please a man 70s style
Value: $11-$19

COLLECTING TIP

Sex, drugs and rock and roll found their way into cookbooks of the 1960s and 70s. Like other mid-century collectibles, this category is continuing on in cookbook collecting circles.

Hunt, Mary

1945
Mary Hunt's Salad Bowl
Hunt, Mary
M. Barrows
Hardcover
102 pages
Cute little cookbook with dressings and salads by the owner of a Minneapolis restaurant
Value: $11-$19

Isola, Antonia

1912
Simple Italian Cookery
Isola, Antonia
Harper & Brothers
Hardcover
68 pages
Linen cover, embossed titles
Original printing
Value: $35-$63

J.R. Watkins Co.

1926
Watkins Cook Book
J.R. Watkins Co.
Stapled booklet
64 pages
Scarce early recipe booklet from the J.R. Watkins Co. Color illustrations. Includes color spread showing Watkins products
Value: $30-$60

1935
Watkins 1868-1935 Almanac And Home Book
J. R. Watkins Co.
Stapled booklet
46 pages
Watkins almanac and home book with home remedies, tips, calendars and many pages of illustrations of Watkins products. Black-and-white photos and color illustrations
Value: $20-$36

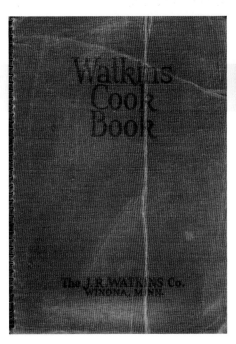

1936
Watkins Cook Book
Allen, Elaine
J. R. Watkins Co.
Soft cover, wire bound
192-plus pages
Value: $27-$48

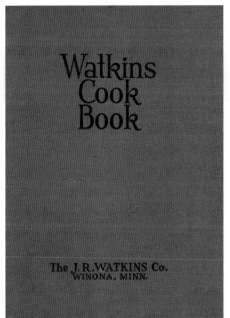

1938-1945
Watkins Cook Book
Allen, Elaine
Whitman
Soft cover, wire bound
Contents of each year are slightly different but covers are similar.
1938: 288 pages, includes a color bird's-eye view of Watkins
buildings
1943: 4th edition, blue cover, 264 pages. No mention of the
war but does have a chapter on economy desserts and one on
economy meats and salads
1948: 288 pages
Wartime edition contains sections on sugar substitutes and
"How to meet the butter shortage," and carries an increased
value of 20-30 percent over that immediately below.
Value: $28-$49

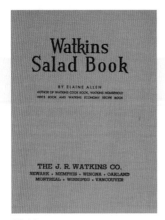

1946
Watkins Salad Book
Allen, Elaine
J. R. Watkins Co.
Hardcover, wire bound
251 pages plus index
Value: $10-$18

1952
Watkins Hearthside Cook Book
Robbins, Ruth
J. R. Watkins Co.
Hardcover
256 pages
Dust jacket folds out to become illustrated kitchen poster with a psalm quote
Value: $34-$61

Dust Jacket

1969, 1981
Waldorf-Astoria Cookbook, The
James, Ted and Cole, Rosalaind
Bramhall House, New York
Hardcover
Recipes and history of the Great American Hotel, the Waldorf-Astoria.
Color and black-and-white photos of the food and the restaurant. Executive chef Eugene Scanlan and Chef Daniel Vigier supervised the selection and testing of the recipes. Ciel Dyer tested recipes at home.
Shown is the 1981 dust jacket and original 1969 first edition blue cover.
Value: $67-$119

Jeffries, Bob

1969
Soul Food Cookbook
Jeffries, Bob
Bobbs Merrill
Hardcover
116 pages
One of the first cookbooks to use the term "soul food."
Value: $32-$56

Kander, Mrs. Simon (Kander, Lizzie Black)

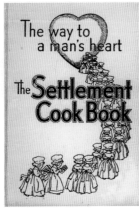 

1936-1947
Settlement Cook Book (The Way To A Man's Heart) Enlarged And Revised
Kander, Mrs. Simon
Hardcover
624 pages
The contents of each printing from 1938-1947 vary slightly. While cover colors vary according to age and condition from white to yellow, the design is the same, making the identification of each edition tricky.
Value: $49-$87

Dust Jacket

Circa 1942
Settlement Cook Book, The
Kander, Mrs. Simon
American Crayon Co.
Hardcover
456 pages
Reprint of the 1910, fourth edition. States "reprint is not published by the Settlement Cook Book Co." on the cover. A Mary Perks book. No copyright date
Printed circa 1942
Value: $25-$44

1954
New Settlement Cook Book, The
Kander, Mrs. Simon
Simon & Schuster
Hardcover
676 pages
Revised and enlarged edition. Some printings of this edition have a blue ribbon on the book cover instead of decoration shown.
Value: $31-$56

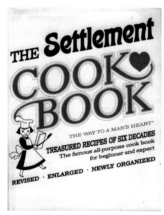

1965
Settlement Cook Book, The
Kander, Mrs. Simon
Simon & Schuster
Hardcover
535 pages
Revised and enlarged
Value: $33-$58

1976
Settlement Cook Book
Kander, Mrs. Simon
Simon & Schuster
Hardcover
757 pages
Third edition. Dust jacket is yellow with stylized cook and large red and black lettering.
Value: $28-$49

Kasdan, Sara

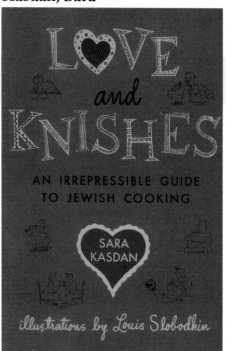

1956
Love And Knishes: An Irrepressible Guide To Jewish Cooking
Kasdan, Sara
The Vanguard Press
Hardcover
191 pages
Illustrations by Louis Slobdodkin
Value: $44-$78

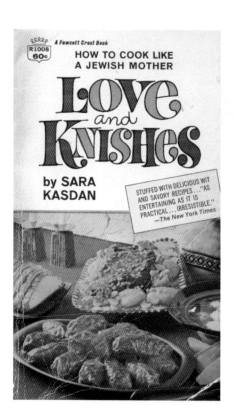

1956
Love And Knishes: How To Cook Like A Jewish Mother
Kasdan, Sara
Fawcett
Paperback
Value: $14-$25

Kaufman, William I.

An accomplished author with over 100 book titles to his name, William I. Kaufman migrated to writing, editing and researching after a lengthy career in television. A born lover of food and wine, he began his professional life by signing on with fledgling network NBC in 1947, doing work as a director, producer and casting director.

His writing career began with a variety of books for fellow directors and aspiring TV personnel, but quickly shifted towards food with 1955's *Cooking With the Experts*, a collection of recipes from televised cooking shows. In 1963 he left television and began to write voraciously on dozens of food related subjects, from nuts to coffee, natural foods to home-style cooking. He even wrote of religious cuisine (his *The Catholic Cook Book: Traditional Feast and Fast Day Recipes*, 1965, is a must for the devout home chef).

Once called the "Salvador Dali of tuna casseroles" (his *Art of Casserole Cookery*, 1967, ventured into the realm of the surreal with dishes like tuna-and-canned-fruit casserole), William ultimately wrote roughly 150 books before his death, though not all were related to food.

1965
I Love Peanut Butter Cookbook, The
Kaufman, William I.
Doubleday & Co.
Hardcover
130 pages
Value: $10-$18

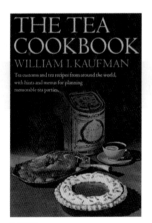

1966
Tea Cookbook, The
Kaufman, William I.
Doubleday
Hardcover
188 pages
Tea customs and tea recipes from around the world with hints and menus for planning memorable tea parties. Black-and-white photos
Value: $9-$16

Keen, Adelaide

1902
With A Saucepan Over The Sea
Keen, Adelaide
Little, Brown and Co.
Hardcover
265 pages plus ads
Subtitled: "Quaint and delicious recipes from the kitchens of foreign countries."
A scarce cookbook investigating the regional cooking of Europe at the turn of the century
Value: $105-$188

Kiene, Julia

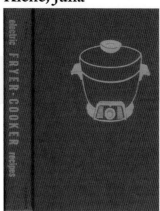

1954
Electric Fryer-Cooker Recipes
Kiene, Julia
Barrows
Hardcover
254 pages
Value: $7-$12

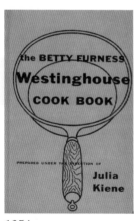 

1954
Betty Furness Westinghouse Cook Book, The
Kiene, Julia
Simon and Schuster
Hardcover
496 pages
Printed with three color covers—brown, aqua and yellow. The contents are the same with the exception of the brown cover, which does not have the short additional section in the back of the book entitled "A Modern Version of the Back of Grandmother's Cookbook."
Value: $26-$46

Kiessling Publishing Co.

1939
Cupid's Book: 1939
Kiessling Publishing Co.
Kiessling Publishing Co.
Soft cover
64 pages
Helpful recipes, measurements and general information for the 1930s bride, including a catalog of household products.
Some versions have coupons for local wedding-related services.
Black-and-white photos and illustrations
Value: $9-$16

Kirk, Dorothy

Dorothy Kirk Singer, a 1940s consultant, editor and author, was one of the home economics movement's most valuable teachers and pioneers. A graduate of Columbia University's Teachers College, she began her career by serving with the Y.M.C.A. Canteen Service during World War I.

After signing on as the food editor at *Woman's Home Companion* magazine, she published the well-known cooking and housekeeping guide *The Woman's Home Companion Cook Book* (1942). The book, one of many "mother" books published to assist women in running the home, sold over 1 million copies and enjoyed over a half dozen printings; it is still recognized by vintage book dealers as one of the most coveted cookbook classics of its time.

1942-1946
Woman's Home Companion Cook Book
Kirk, Dorothy and Roberts, Willa (editors)
P. F. Collier & Son Corp.
Hardcover
952 pages
First edition is shown here in rare, original 1942 wartime dust jacket. 1942-1945 printings contain a short wartime postscript addressing the "inevitable food shortages." While this exact cookbook was reprinted many times between 1942 and 1955, only the first 1942 printing mentions Willa Roberts as the co-editor.
Color and black-and-white photos and illustrations
Value: $67-$119

1946
Woman's Home Companion Cook Book
Kirk, Dorothy (editor)
Garden City Publishing
Hardcover
952 pages
Value: $60-$106

1946
Woman's Home Companion Cook Book
Kirk, Dorothy (editor)
Garden City Publishing
Hardcover
952 pages
Cover varies from green to blue or black.
Value: $60-$106

1950-1955
Woman's Home Companion Cook Book
Kirk, Dorothy
P.F. Collier & Son
Hardcover
987 pages
Same cover design as 1940s cream cover and the main body of cookbook remains the same as earlier printing, however additional chapters have been added at end of book for this edition.
Value: $67-$119

Ladies' Home Journal

One of America's longest running publications, *Ladies' Home Journal* began as a simple newspaper supplement written by a publisher's wife for the late 1800s paper *Tribune and Farmer*. The humble column, titled the "Ladies Home Journal and Practical Housekeeper," and written by Louisa Knapp in 1883, soon grew into a thicker women's monthly publication with a shorter title and circulation in the thousands (and eventually, millions) and has been in print for well over a century.

Originally covering news, politics, women's issues, parenting, beauty, fashion, cooking and nutrition, the *Journal* frequently impressed literary circles with focused essays and reviews, short works of fiction and poetry. The work of Rudyard Kipling and other literary notables appeared in its pages.

Now one of Meredith Corp.'s most read publications, the magazine bills itself as a supporter of family life, values, public health and personal development, and still features the cooking tips and recipes that helped secure its audience.

See also: Cookbooks: Truax, Carol.

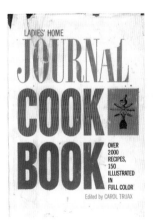

1963
Ladies' Home Journal Cookbook
Truax, Carol (editor)
Doubleday
Hardcover
728 pages
1st and second printing of this cookbook have the exact same contents. However, the covers are different, the endpapers have different illustrations and the first printing is thumb-indexed.
Value: $45-$81

1964
Ladies' Home Journal Dessert Cookbook
Truax, Carol (editor)
Doubleday
Hardcover
280 pages
Value: $11-$19

Lasswell, Mary

Mrs. Erna Rasmussen loved a good frothy mug of beer. She loved it so much, in fact, that she wrote a cookbook specifically for those beer mavens unable to part with their glasses long enough to prepare a proper meal. The resulting publication, 1946's *Mrs. Rasmussen's Book of One-Arm Cookery*, is now the definitive guide to cooking while intoxicated.

However, the inebriated author was unable to take the credit for her guide, as she was all a figment of author Mary Lasswell's imagination.

Mrs. Rasmussen, a widow and dedicated home cook, was one of three lovable old ladies in Lasswell's 1942 novel *Suds in Your Eye*. The humorous book, illustrated by famed New Yorker artist George Price, was the first in a popular series about food, beer and life-loving elderly friends living out their twilight years with vigor. Filled with Mrs. Rasmussen's advice and brew-related cooking techniques, the resulting *Book of One-Armed Cookery* showcased beer-friendly, easy to make dishes such as huevos rancheros, beef and kidney pie, Mexican tripe and roast duck. *Suds in Your Eye* was later adapted into a Broadway play, bringing Mrs. Rasmussen and her cookery to new, moderately sober audiences.

1946
Mrs. Rasmussen's Book Of One-Arm Cookery
Lasswell, Mary
Houghton Mifflin
Hardcover
102 pages
Illustrations by George Price
Value: $41-$73

Leone, Gene

Gene Leone, son of "Mama Leone" (Luisa Leone) of New York's Leone's Restaurant, helped to build his mother's homey, 24-seat neighborhood restaurant into a New York Theater District landmark that would eventually serve 6,000 customers a night.

1967

Leone's Italian Cookbook
Leone, Gene
Harper & Row
Hardcover
244 pages
Value: $35-$62

Levinson, Leonard

1949

Brown Derby Cookbook, The
Levinson, Leonard
Brown Derby
Hardcover
Shown is the first edition specially bound and published for Brown Derby Restaurant customers.
The later 50th anniversary edition was printed circa 1976 and valued at $20-40.
Value: $60-$106

Liberace, Wladziu Valentino

1970

Liberace Cooks!

Liberace, Wladziu Valentino (with Truax, Carol)
Doubleday
Hardcover
225 pages
Wladziu Valentino Liberace
Part biography, part cookbook, it includes hundreds of recipes from Liberace's Polish and Italian roots. Color photos of Liberace cooking
Value: $69-$123

Lincoln, Mary J. (aka Mrs. D.A. Lincoln)

A Massachusetts native who, along with contemporaries Maria Parloa and Fannie Farmer, contributed to the great New England food movement that helped change cookery in America, Mrs. Mary Lincoln was a happy and unassuming housewife with no aspirations to change the culinary landscape of a nation. However, when her husband fell ill in the late 1860s, Mrs. Lincoln was pushed out into the workforce, putting her on course to write one of the greatest books (cooking related or not) of the 19th century.

A solid homemaker and graduate of Wheaton Female Seminary, Mary joined the teaching staff at the Boston Cooking School and served as principal for six years, starting in 1879. Soon after, in 1884, she wrote her *Boston Cook Book*, which became an immediate success based on its logical organization of recipes and techniques, easy readability and dedication to cookery as an art.

The book went on to enjoy dozens of printings, and was recognized in 1946 by The Grolier Club as one of the greatest books of the 1800s. The Grolier Club, as well as many others, declared Fannnie Farmer's own celebrated book of the same city a direct offshoot of Mary's work. The book went on to be a standard teaching text in many home economics and culinary schools.

Additional books by Mrs. Lincoln:
Carving and Serving
Boston School Kitchen Text Book— Lessons in cooking for the use of teachers and classes in public and industrial schools.
Peerless Cookbook
Twenty Lessons in Cookery—Compiled from the *Boston School Kitchen Text Book* and printed on tinted cards. The set includes about 150 cooking receipts and one card of rules for general housework. They were used in the industrial and public school cooking classes in Boston, New Haven, Brooklyn, Pittsburgh, Milwaukee and other cities.
Frozen Dainties
Home Science Cook Book (co-authored by Anna Barrows)

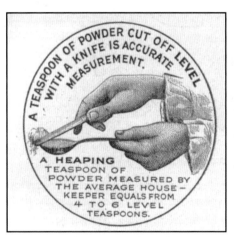

An advertisement for Mrs. Lincoln's Baking Powder in 1880s *Mrs. Lincoln's Boston Cook Book.*

1880s-1890s
Mrs. Lincoln's Boston Cook Book
Lincoln, Mary J.
Little, Brown & Co.
Hardcover
536 pages plus 24 ads
Showing early edition with title page missing. Brown cloth with marbled, pastedown decoration on front and back covers. Sometimes erroneously described as half-leather or brown cloth over marbled boards
24 period advertisements plus 22-24 blank pages at end of book
Value: $63-$112

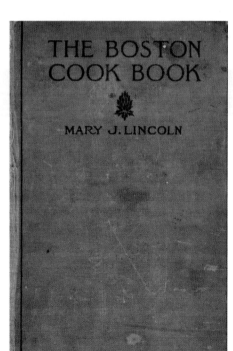

1908, 1913
Mrs. Lincoln's Boston Cook Book
Lincoln, Mary J.
Little, Brown & Co.
Hardcover
578 pages plus ads
Cover title: *The Boston Cook Book*
Value: $45-$81

Lucas, Dione

The woman credited with paving the way for Julia Child, who called Lucas "the Mother of French Cooking in America," and countless female culinary greats to follow, Dione Lucas was and is one of the most important figures in recent culinary history. Daughter of the British artist Henry Wilson, Dione was the first woman to graduate from the prestigious L'Ecole du Cordon Bleu in Paris and complete a formal chef's apprenticeship at the restaurant Drouant—no small accomplishments for a woman in the testosterone-charged world of professional kitchens.

She went on to become an accomplished chef, feeding celebrities and world leaders (including Adolph Hitler) alike before moving to New York City, where she opened restaurants such as the Cordon Bleu Restaurant and School and The Egg Basket, the latter of which is frequently credited with cementing America's love of omelets. Having founded the cooking school Le Petit Cordon Bleu in London before her move to the States, Dione continued her focus on culinary education in New York with her NYC-based Cordon Bleu School and various intimate cooking classes.

Starting in the 1940s, she followed Ida Bailey Allen's footsteps by hosting cooking shows (*To a Queen's Taste, The Dione Lucas Cooking Show,* etc.) on television. Her books, including the *Cordon Bleu Cook Book* and *The Gourmet Cooking School Cook Book,* remain invaluable resources for French cookery enthusiasts today.

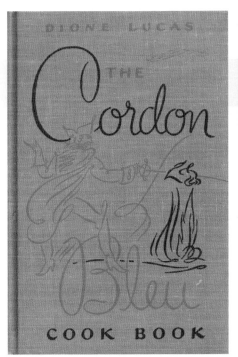

Dust Jacket

1947
Cordon Bleu Cook Book, The
Lucas, Dione
Little, Brown & Co.
Hardcover
321 pages
Black-and-white illustrations by Phoebe Nicol
Value: $17-$31

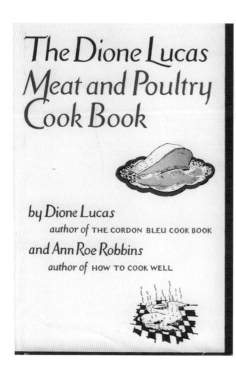

1955
Dione Lucas Meat And Poultry Cook Book, The
Lucas, Dione and Robbins,
Ann Roe
Gramercy
Hardcover
324 pages
Drawings by Phoebe Nicol
Value: $16-$28

Mardikian, George

1944
Dinner At Omar Khayyam's
Mardikian, George
Viking Press
Hardcover
150 pages
Value: $27-$48

Marie, Tante

Tante Marie's cornerstone cookbook, *La Veritable Cuisine de Famille*, has been a staple in French homes since 1903. There really was no "Tante Marie"—the name was fabricated by the author/publisher to make her cookbooks sound homey. The recipes (some of which are likely centuries old) were actually collected from convents and monasteries.

1949-1959
Tante Marie's French Kitchen
Marie, Tante
Oxford University Press
Hardcover
323 pages
Translation of the *French La Veritable Cuisine de Famille par Tante Marie*
Value: $25-$44

1954
Tante Marie's French Pastry
Marie, Tante and
Turgeon, Charlotte (translator)
Oxford University Press
Hardcover
146 pages
Translated from the French by Charlotte Turgeon
Value: $39-$69

Masterton, Elsie

A poignant biography of this Blueberry Hill (Goshen, Vermont) innkeeper and restaurateur, Elsie Masterton, can be found in daughter Laurie's biography *Elsie's Biscuits: Simple Stories of Me, My Mother and Food.*

Additional cookbooks by Elsie Masterton:

The Blueberry Hill Cookbook
Blueberry Hill Kitchen Notes

COLLECTING TIP

Owners of small bed and breakfasts, farmhouses and country inns have written many fine cookbooks. Sometimes gourmet, sometimes down-home, these texts are included in a popular collector's category we call "restaurant cookbooks."

1963
Blueberry Hill Menu Cookbook
Masterton, Elsie
Thomas Y. Crowell Co.
Hardcover
373 pages
Second cookbook by Elsie Masterton, a 1950s innkeeper and restaurant chef of the Blueberry Hill Inn, Vermont. Jacket design by Ava Morgan. Book illustrations by the author
Value: $12-$21

McBride, Mary Margaret

Best known for her notable contribution to broadcast journalism, Missouri native Mary Margaret McBride was a food lover with comfortable, no-nonsense appeal. A talented journalist, Mary wrote for *The Cleveland Press and Evening Mail* before she began broadcasting from New York in 1934. Her ease on air soon led to her own show, an afternoon broadcast that discussed food, recipes, housekeeping tips, interviews and a variety of timely topics.

A patron of the authentic, she actually ate food on the air, sensuously describing culinary treats to millions of tuned-in listeners (over 18,000 of whom packed Madison Square Garden to see her in 1944). Additionally, her well-honed interviewing skills attracted some of the biggest names in entertainment and politics, and legitimized the broadcast to non-housewives and even men.

During her tenure, Bob Hope, Eleanor Roosevelt and Jimmy Durante all made appearances on the show. Throughout, she maintained her integrity by endorsing only the products she truly loved and used.

Neither of the encyclopedic cookbooks bearing her name mentions her contribution in the credits and we are unsure if she simply lent her name to the project or was responsible for the recipes.

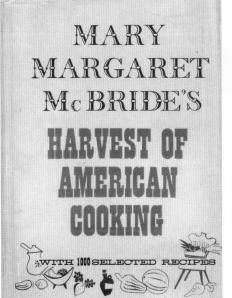

1957
Mary Margaret Mcbride's Harvest Of American Cooking
McBride, Mary Margaret
G. P. Putnam's Sons
Hardcover
453 pages
Spot color illustrations
Value: $25-$44

1958
Mary Margaret Mcbride Encyclopedia Of Cooking Set
London, Anne (editor)
Homemakers Research Institute
Hardcover
Set of 12 volumes. Later reprinted and sold as individual loose-leaf sections to make up the "Deluxe Illustrated Edition."
Color and black-and-white photos and illustrations
Value: $67-$119

1960
Mary Margaret Mcbride Encyclopedia Of Cooking Deluxe Illustrated Edition
London, Anne (editor)
Homemaker's Research Institute
Hardcover
Screw-post binding holds individual loose-leaf sections. Gigantic volume means binding often suffers from the weight of the cookbook; a professional repair is acceptable, detracting little from the value.
Black-and-white photos and illustrations
Value: $67-$150

McCall's

A monthly magazine founded in the late 1870s, shortly before competitor *Ladies' Home Journal* appeared, McCall's was yet another long-running women's magazine with a strong literary slant. Focusing on cooking, kitchen tips, parenting, homemaking, home decor and fashion, the magazine frequently published legitimate essays and fiction alongside articles on the household arts. The magazine's encyclopedic 1970s cookbook, available in a range of colors, remains highly desirable.

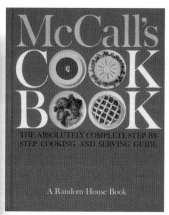

1963
McCall's Cook Book
Random House
Hardcover
786 pages
Same contents available in green, yellow, red or blue cover
Value: $36-$64

M1

McCall's COOKIE COLLECTION

COOKIES WITH CHARACTER

COOKIES THAT KEEP

COOKIES-IN-A-HURRY FROM DO-AHEAD DOUGH

COOKIES THAT CARRY

COOKIES THAT PACK

COOKIES TO CAPTURE THE IMAGINATION

COOKIES GRANDMA NEVER MADE

PLUS: COOKIER COOKIES FOR GOODIER GIVING

The soft cover cookbooks
M1. *Cookie Collection*
M2. *Casserole Collection*
M3. *Practically Cookless Cookbook*
M4. *Salads & Salad Dressings*
M5. *Book of Cakes and Pies*
M6. *Book of Marvelous Meats*
M7. *Dessert Discoveries*
M8. *Family-Style Cookbook*
M9. *Company Cookbook*
M10. *Do-Ahead Party Book*
M11. *Coast-to-coast Cooking*
M12. *Worldwide Cooking*
M13. *Fish N' Fowl Cookbook*
M14. *Show-off Cookbook*
M15. *Cocktail Time Cookbook*
M16. *Home-baked Breads*
M17. *Book of Merry Eating*
M18. *Picnic and Patio Cookbook*
Index and Recipe Reminder

1965-1975
McCall's Cookbook Series

Editors of *McCall's*
Advance Publishers
Series of 18 (plus index) large-format, soft cover cookbooks.
Originally available with a white plastic holder
Complete set with holder: $95-$120

COLLECTING TIP

Some collect books for their design aspects, such as the simple geometrics of 30s art deco, or the mod pop and op art patterns and colors of the swingin' '60s.

1967
Redbook's Casserole Cookbook
McCall's
McCall
Soft cover, comb binding
96 pages
Illustrated by Abe Gurvin
Value: $9-$16

Mead, Harriet Morgan

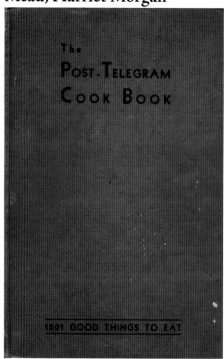

1934
Post-Telegram Cook Book, The
Mead, Harriet Morgan
Fost
Hardcover
380 pages
Recipes contributed from readers of *The Bridgeport Post, The Bridgeport Telegram* and the *Bridgeport Sunday Post*.
Recipes attributed to contributors
Value: $45-$81

Meade, Martha

The face and spokesperson for General Mill's Sperry Flour line of baking and cooking products, Martha Meade was known for her recipe books, pamphlets, short food and cooking articles, the occasional cooking class, and for running the Sperry Division's test kitchens. She was also entirely fictional. In fact, the name "Martha Meade" was actually a registered trademark of the General Mills Co.

Her published works, including the 1939 *Martha Meade's Modern Meal Maker* (which billed her as "the West's favorite cooking counselor and famous radio lecturer"), *Martha Meade's Failure Proof Recipes* (1958), and *Recipes from the Old South* (1961), can be attributed to the dedicated employees of General Mills. Her articles, pamphlets and recipes were peppered with cheery ad-speak that directly endorsed the Sperry line of products. However, despite Martha's lack of journalistic integrity, many of her recipes were indeed "failure proof."

See also Recipe Booklets: Sperry Flour.

1935
Modern Meal Maker
Meade, Martha
Sperry Flour Co.
Hardcover, wire bound
428 pages plus index
Tab indexed by month
1,115 menus, 744 recipes plus 2,000 "recipe-ettes" organized by each day of the year. Homemaking hints and special calendar day menus
Value: $32-$56

Mercantile Publishing Co.

1893
Our Home Cyclopedia, The
Author not noted
Mercantile Publishing Co.
Hardcover
400 pages
Black and white engravings. Bitting cites author as Edgar S. Darling [Anon.]
Value: $67-$119

Merchants Specialty Co.

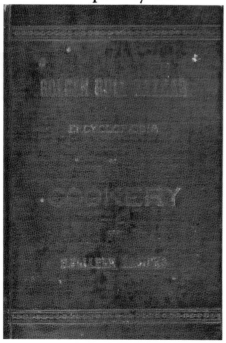

1892
Golden Rule Bazaar Encyclopaedia Of Cookery And Reliable Recipes
Merchants Specialty Co.
Hardcover
400 pages
Cookbook printed expressly for the patrons of the Golden Rule Bazaar of San Francisco and Portland, Ore. The Bazaar merged with the Emporium—a San Francisco department store founded as a co-operative of individually owned shops—in 1897. Along with recipes like Salted Beef (keeps for years) and Pigeons in Jelly, there are chapters with recipes for cosmetics, medicines, wines and perfumes.
Approximately 400 pages
A few black and white charts and illustrations of meat cuts
Value: $550-$981

Merriman, Beth

1953
Bridgeport Sunday Post Parade Cook Book
Merriman, Beth
Parade
Soft cover
108 pages
Color and black-and-white photos and illustrations
Value: $32-$56

Mitchell, Jan

1952-1956
Luchow's German Cookbook
Mitchell, Jan
Doubleday & Co.
Hardcover
224 pages
Illustrations by Ludwig Bemelmans
Luchow's Restaurant in New York City opened its doors in 1882, and was frequented by prominent personalities in the arts, politics and society.
Value: $27-$48

Mitchell, Margaret

The 1930s director of the Wear-Ever test kitchens and head of the Alcoa Wrap kitchens, Margaret Mitchell was responsible for everything from market research to product development and cookbook production. Her extensive, hands-on research of how cookware was used lead to the development of specific utensils for the newly introduced electric range. Mitchell proposed efficient utensils with straight sides in specific sizes and diameters that precisely fit the range burners.

1951
Margaret Mitchell's Mealtime Magic Meat And Poultry Cookery
Mitchell, Margaret
Wear-Ever
Hardcover
120 pages
Volume 1 of a series. Spot color illustrations
Value: $18-$31

1951
Margaret Mitchell's Mealtime Magic Desserts
Mitchell, Margaret
Wear-Ever
Hardcover
127 pages
Volume 2 of a series
Introduction includes a photo of Margaret Mitchell.
Black-and-white photos and spot color illustrations
Value: $25-$44

1961
Cutco Cook Book
Mitchell, Margaret
Wear-ever Aluminum Cutco Division
Hardcover
128 pages
Line illustrations by Frank Marcello
Value: $4-$8

1964
Margaret Mitchell's Mealtime Magic Cookbook
Mitchell, Margaret
Pocket
Paperback
309 pages
Sensational secrets of aluminum wrap cookery
Value: $4-$8

Murphy, Agnes

Dust Jacket

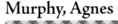

1955
American Everyday Cookbook, The
Murphy, Agnes
Random
Hardcover
Un-paginated. Recipes numbered through #1,998.
Inexpensive paper and glued binding makes this hard to find in good condition.
Value: $20-$36

Myerson, Dorothy

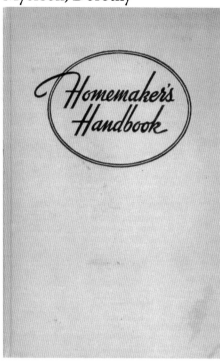

1935
Homemaker's Handbook
Myerson, Dorothy
Whittlesey
Hardcover
566 pages
Complete homemaker's guide
Value: $34-$61

Mystery Chef

1941
Mystery Chef's Own Cook Book, The
MacPherson, John
Blakiston
Hardcover
366 pages
Revised with additional recipes and new dust jacket
Value: $35-$62

1949
Never Fail Cook Book, The
MacPherson, John
Garden City
Hardcover
190 pages
Value: $16-$28

Neil, Marion Harris

B orn in the British Isles, Marion Harris Neil, of Scottish descent, carved herself a comfortable niche in the United States as a food, homemaking and recipe expert and writer. An authority who preached the gospel of method, good sense and discipline when it came to household duties, Marion's writings on home-related subjects, from dusting to managing expenses, appeared in various national newspapers, including *The Chicago Daily Tribune* and *The New York Times*.

She also worked as Cookery Editor for the venerable *Ladies' Home Journal* in the years leading up and into the 1920s. Her editing and recipe exposure helped to fuel several popular cookbooks and recipe collections, including *Canning, Preserving, and Pickling* (1914), *The Something-Different Dish* (1915), and *Mrs. Neil's Cooking Secrets* (1924).

Her best-known book, however, was published by Proctor and Gamble during Marion's time as an endorser for the revolutionary new product Crisco. Alternately titled *A Calendar of Dinners With 615 Recipes*, her *Story of Crisco* (1913) helped introduce the innovative shortening to thousands of dinner tables as an invaluable ingredient for sautéing, baking, frying and stewing.

See also: Recipe Booklets, Ryzon.

1916
Calendar Of Dinners, A
Neil, Marion Harris
Crisco
Hardcover
231 pages
Early promo cookbook for Crisco that includes the history/ story of Crisco
615 recipes and a menu for each day of the year
The 11th edition is shown. Black-and-white illustrations
Value: $23-$41

1923-1924
Mrs. Neil's Cooking Secrets
Neil, Marion Harris
Proctor and Gamble
Stapled booklet
128 pages
Original version shown. The 2001 reprint has no substantial resale value.
Value: $25-$44

Noble, Ruth V.

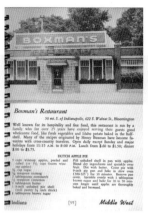

1955
Guide To Distinctive Dining
Noble, Ruth V.
Berkshire
Paperback
144 pages
Recipes and photos of restaurants across the country
Value: $17-$31

Osborn, Marjorie Noble

1934
Jolly Times Cook Book
Osborn, Marjorie Noble
Rand McNally
Hardcover
64 pages
Illustrated by Clarence Biers
Value: $21-$38

Pacific Trading Co.

1928
Mandarin Chop Suey Cook Book
Pacific Trading Co.
Soft cover
96 pages
Early cookbook from the Pacific Trading Co. of Chicago with recipes for Chinese dishes. Claims to be the "first and only book of its character published in the English language containing genuine recipes of famous Chinese chefs."
Value: $35-$62

Paddleford, Clementine

A woman once described by *Time* magazine as "the best known food editor in the United States," Clementine Paddleford had a voracious appetite for all things edible. The noted 20th-century food writer was famous for her verbose and sensual descriptions of epicurean items, and spun simple food descriptions into veritable love sonnets to food.

Clementine wrote for numerous publications including *This Week*, *Gourmet*, *Farm and Fireside*, *The New York Sun* and *The New York Herald Tribune*, and was known as a tenacious and talented reporter who would stop at nothing to get her story—she learned to fly a plane in order to travel for stories more efficiently.

Called by *The New York Times* "the Nellie Bly of culinary journalism," the writer sailed the high seas to learn how fishermen ate, traveled to Britain for Queen Elizabeth's coronation lunch, and sampled lobster (for just $1.75 a half) at the World's Fair (1939). While her journalism skills may have matched her zest for life, her cooking ability, however, did not—Clementine hated to cook, and preferred describing meals to preparing them.

1960
How America Eats
Paddleford, Clementine
Charles Scribner and Sons
Hardcover
496 pages
Long considered one of the most thorough and interesting American regional cookbook compilations. Paddleford writes in a warm and engaging style, recounting stories of personal encounters with cooks around the country, faithfully penning their recipes and capturing their spirit.
Twelve years in the making, Paddleford's book is a charming read and an American treasure. Color and black and white photos
Value: $67-$119

1966
Clementine Paddleford's Cook Young Cookbook
Paddleford, Clementine
Pocket Books
Paperback
124 pages
Selection of the best "quick-and-easy" recipes from a nationwide recipe swap instituted by Paddleford for her "How America Eats" series in *This Week Magazine*.
Value: $11-$19

1970
Best In American Cooking, The
Paddleford, Clementine
Charles Scribner and Sons
Hardcover
312 pages
Recipes in this book also appeared in *How America Eats*.
Value: $24-$43

Parloa, Maria

One of several great cooking influences to emerge from New England in the late 1800s, Maria Parloa was a popular home economics expert, teacher and accomplished chef. As a professional with pastry expertise, she worked for a time as hotel chef/baker in the Northeast, including at Appledore, a seasonal resort off the coast of Maine with significant literary provenance (Emerson and Harriet Beecher Stowe were guests). Her time at the resort led to *The Appledore Cook Book* (1873), a recipe book that set in motion her long career in cookery.

A contemporary of Fannie Farmer and Mary Lincoln, Maria too had a talent for teaching, lecturing on cooking in New England and working with the Women's Education Assoc. before opening her own cooking schools in Boston, 1880, and in New York, 1882. Despite the misconception that she helped found the revered Boston Cooking School, there is no evidence that Maria was involved with its creation, although she taught at the establishment in 1879.

A stickler for organization and the right ingredients, Maria's books frequently discussed how to run house and home efficiently. The best known of these was *Miss Parloa's New Cookbook: A Guide to Marketing and Cookery* (1881). Written to simplify the often overwhelming and intimidating task of market shopping, it set the stage for another meticulous guide for housewives, *An Ideal Kitchen: Miss Parloa's Kitchen Companion: A Guide for All Who Would Be Good Housekeepers* (1887).

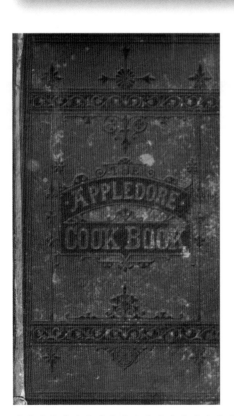

1880
Appledore Cook Book, The
Parloa, Maria
Andrew F. Graves
Hardcover
240 pages
Second edition
Value: $105-$188

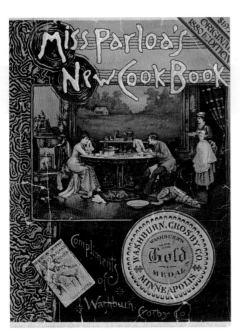

1978
Miss Parloa's New Cook Book
Parloa, Maria
General Mills
Soft cover
72 pages
Facsimile reprint of an 1880s Washburn-Crosby version of Miss Parloa's cookbook.
Desirable for its preservation of the history of the original cookbook, it includes directions for browning a soufflé with a hot shovel. Black and white illustrations
Value: $11-$19

Pechin, Mary Shelley

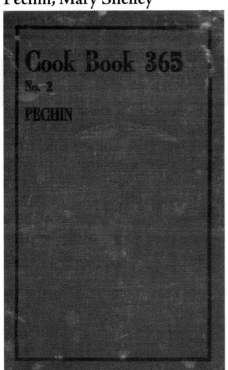

1915
Cook Book 365 No. 2
Pechin, Mary Shelley
Burrows Bros.
Hardcover
370 pages
Early and obscure cookbook with basic cooking instruction and some unusual recipes like Savarin with Rum, Grated Quince Marmalade, and Clove Cake. Additional section with cleaning and cosmetic recipes
Value: $46-$81

Peck, Paula

Praised by *The New York Times*' Craig Claiborne in 1966 as "one of the most remarkable talents in the world of food today," Paula Peck was best known as an outstanding baker and author of, appropriately, *The Art of Fine Baking* (1961). She was one of the respected darlings of the budding 1960s mainstream food industry, hired frequently to cook for celebrities and other well-known cooking professionals, such as the venerable James Beard (who praised the *Art of Fine Baking* as one of the best baking books ever written, a statement that goes largely unchallenged even today).

When *Art of Good Cooking* was released in 1966, Claiborne gave it a glowing review, pointing out that Peck's experience as a professional chef made her recipes (in this case, a far reaching variety of American recipes diverse enough to include both Jewish chicken livers and Mexican-style chicken) refreshingly reliable. His adept observation explains why both books have remained staples on many professional and home cooks' shelves for almost 50 years.

Paula died young at only 45, just six years after the release of her second book, denying both her contemporaries and future generations access to her brilliant culinary skills.

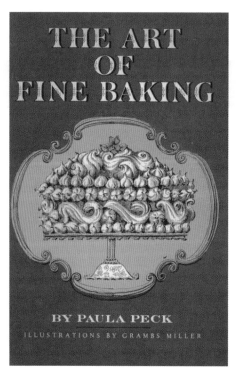

1961
Art Of Fine Baking, The
Peck, Paula
Simon and Schuster
Hardcover
320 pages
Attractively illustrated by Grambs Miller. Black-and-white illustrations. Jacket design by Hal Fiedler
Value: $20-$35

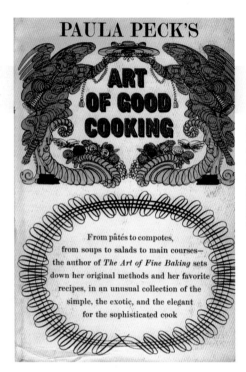

1966
Paula Peck's The Art Of Good Cooking
Peck, Paula
Simon and Schuster
Hardcover
368 pages
Value: $25-$40

Peerless

1960
Book Of Famous Old New Orleans Recipes, A
Author not noted
Peerless
Soft cover, plastic comb
Over 300 authentic Creole recipes used in the South for more than 200 years and " ... culled from old files and extracted from the yellowed pages of many a Creole family's treasured recipe book."
Undated circa 1960
Black-and-white illustrations. Some copies have translucent paper wrapper.
Value: $12-$21

Penny, Prudence

Prudence Penny's west coast home radio show ran for approximately 20 years. Yet, despite the popularity of her show and the cookbooks and newspaper columns in her name, reliable information about her creation and identity remains elusive. Like "Aunt Sammy," Prudence was likely a fictional home economist, offering household hints, recipes and advice on the radio and in local papers. We suspect different individuals penned her cookbooks.

She is credited as a columnist for the *Seattle Post Intelligencer* and for the *San Francisco Examiner*, and as Home Economics Editor for the *Los Angeles Times*.

Some of the names associated with Prudence Penny:

Hazeltine, Alyce
Goldberg, Hyman
Houghton, Allene Gregory
Carillo, Leo

1935, 1936
Cosmopolitan Seattle
Penny, Prudence
Post-Intelligencer, Seattle
Stapled Booklet
48 pages
Recipes from local Seattle Restaurants circa 1936
Many black and white photos of local chefs. Presented to the Founder Members of the *Seattle Post-Intelligencer* Homemakers' Club
Value: $39-$69

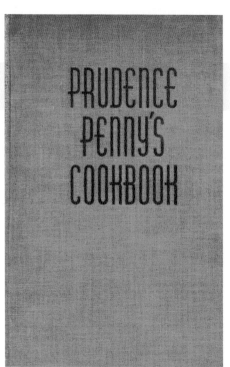

1939
Prudence Penny's Cookbook
Penny, Prudence
Prentice-Hall
Hardcover
385 pages
By Prudence Penny, Home Economics Editor of the *Los Angeles Examiner*
Adept black-and-white cartoon illustrations. Photo of and intro by the actor Leo Carillo
Value: $52-$93

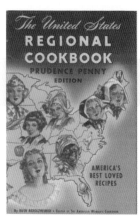
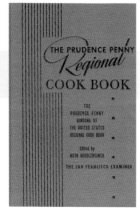

1940-1956
Prudence Penny Regional Cook Book (Aka The United States Regional Cookbook)
Berolzheimer, Ruth (editor)
Consolidated Book Publishers
Hardcover
752 pages
Prudence Penny's cookbook in name only. This is a version of *The United States Regional Cookbook* edited by Ruth Berolzheimer. Color and black-and-white photos and illustrations. Thumb-indexed. Cover colors and dates may vary but contents are the same.
Value: $34-$61

1943
Prudence Penny's Coupon Cookery
Penny, Prudence
Murray & Gee
Hardcover
128 pages
A guide to good meals under wartime conditions of rationing and food shortages.
Black and white cartoon-style illustrations
Value: $27-$48

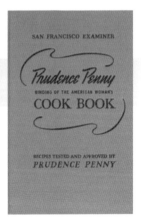

1952-1957
San Francisco Examiner Prudence Penny Binding Of The American Woman's Cook Book
Berolzheimer, Ruth (editor)
Consolidated Book Publishers
Hardcover
856 pages
Prudence Penny's cookbook in name only. This is a version of the *The American Woman's Cookbook*, edited by Ruth Berolzheimer.
Thumb-indexed. Color and black-and-white photos and illustrations
Value: $31-$56

Peter Pauper Press

Peter Beilenson and wife Edna started Peter Pauper Press in their Mount Vernon, N.Y., basement in 1928. The small, attractive volumes cover a wide range of subjects from poetry to puzzles. The cookbook collection began circa 1950 and was the brainchild of Edna, who initiated the decorative cloth bindings with sweet illustrations and simple recipes that appeal to collectors.

Double the price shown if found in original box.

Further Reading:

Recalling Peter: The Life and Times of Peter Beilenson and his Peter Pauper Press, edited by Paul A. Bennett, New York: The Typophiles, 1964

Additional Titles

Holiday Punches, Party Bowls and Soft Drinks
The Holiday Cookbook
Cooking to Kill: The Poison Cookbook
The ABC of Casseroles
The ABC of Chafing Dish Cookery
ABC of Herb & Spice Cookery
Abalone to Zabaglione
The ABC of Barbecue
The ABC of Cookies
The Melting Pot
Simple Viennese Cookery
ABC Of Cheese Cookery
ABC of Gourmet Cookery
Christmas Stocking Book
ABC of Jiffy Cookery
Simple Continental Cookery
Holiday Cookies
Holiday Candies
Holiday Goodies and How to Make Them
Merrie Christmas Cook Book
Merrie Christmas Drink Book
Queen of Hearts Cook Book
Recipes Mother Used to Make

1954
ABC of Casseroles, The
Peter Pauper Press
Hardcover
61 pages
Value: $3-$6

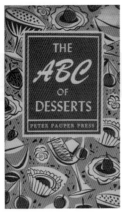

1958
ABC of Desserts, The
Peter Pauper Press
Hardcover
62 pages
Illustrations by Ruth McCrea
Value: $10-$18

1958
ABC of Salads, The
Peter Pauper Press
Hardcover
62 pages
Illustrations by Ruth McCrea
Value: $6-$11

COLLECTING TIP

Books by certain publishers are collected, no matter the subject matter. Cookbooks produced by Ward-Ritchie Press, Peter Pauper Press and Penguin are just a few examples.

1958
ABC of Wine Cookery, The
Peter Pauper Press
Hardcover
62 pages
Value: $9-$16

1963
Simple Continental Cookery
Beilenson, Edna (editor)
Peter Pauper Press
Hardcover
60 pages
Illustrations by Ruth McCrea
Value: $9-$16

1964
Simple Hawaiian Cookery
Beilenson, Edna (editor)
Peter Pauper Press
Hardcover
62 pages
Decorations by Ruth McCrea
Value: $10-$18

Piggly Wiggly

Circa 1925
Piggly Wiggly All Over The World Cook Book
Piggly Wiggly
Soft cover
224 pages
A collection of recipes "by the finest chefs and cooking kitchens in the United States," prepared for The Piggly Wiggly shopper
Ads from food manufacturers throughout. Not dated.
Appears to be published in the '20s
Value: $41-$73

Pillsbury, Ann

One of several mythical marketing characters created by the advertising team of what is now known as General Mills Inc., Ann Pillsbury was billed as an all-American, cheery, common sense baking and home cookery expert. In actuality, she was simply a name that represented the efforts of the Pillsbury Home Service Department.

Like Martha Meade, Aunt Jenny and Betty Crocker, she was the embodiment of all things middle-America, a sympathetic character with whom average homemakers could relate. Appearing for the first time in the mid 1940s, she was credited with roughly a dozen books and pamphlets on baking and cookery, all of which utilized Pillsbury products in one form or another.

Books like *Ann Pillsbury's Sugar Shy Recipes* and *Ann Pillsbury's Meat Miser Magic* (1944) were published appropriately to assist with mandatory wartime rationing, while later compilations, such as *Bake the No-Knead Way: Ann Pillsbury's Amazing Discoveries* (1946) simply encouraged women to get in the kitchen and bake.

In 1948 a series of popular pamphlets with themed recipes, like "Fun with Breads" and "Fun with Cookies," were released under the title *Ann Pillsbury's Tasty Talk*. In later years, Pillsbury phased out the use of the Ann Pillsbury name until she drifted into obscurity.

Unlike her contemporaries, an artist's rendering or portrait of Ann was never published. The only piece of her identity shared with consumers was her signature.

See also Recipe Booklets, Pillsbury

1933
Balanced Recipes By Pillsbury
Ames, Mary Ellis
Pillsbury
Binder
238 pages
Art deco aluminum box container cover
Value: $48-$86

1952
300 Pillsbury Prize Recipes
Pillsbury
Dell
Paperback
383 pages
Prize winners in the three Pillsbury Grand National 100,000-recipe and baking contests
Value: $13-$23

1954
Ann Pillsbury's New Cook Book
Pillsbury, Ann
Arco
Hardcover
144 pages
Value: $32-$56

1959

Pillsbury's Best 1,000 Recipes: Best Of The Bake-Off Collection

Pillsbury, Ann (editor)
Consolidated Book Publishers
Hardcover
608 pages
Each recipe is a famous Bake-off prizewinner. Includes a history of the Bake-off, color and black-and-white photos of the dishes and illustrations by Suzanne Snider
Shown: Pictorial cover or dust jacket and cloth cover with gold lettering. Cloth cover is billed as the "deluxe edition" and is thumb-indexed. Also available as a souvenir leatherette edition presented to Bake-off winners.
Value: $105-$188

1960s

Pillsbury's Bake-Off Cookbook Series

Pillsbury
Hardcover series/set with the following books:
Pillsbury's Bake Off Cookie Book
Pillsbury's Bake off Main Dish Cook Book
Pillsbury's Breads Cook Book
Pillsbury's Cake Cook Book
Pillsbury's Money Saving Meals
Pillsbury's Meat Cook Book
Pillsbury's Family Weight Control Cook Book
Pillsbury's Entertainment Idea Handbook
Value: $10-$18

1963
Pillsbury Family Cook Book, The
Pillsbury
Hardcover or binder
576
Available in binder and hardcover formats. Same contents as blue and yellow cover but not quite as popular. Color and black-and-white photos and illustrations
Value: $25-$44

Platt, June

1971
June Platt's New England Cook Book
Platt, June
Atheneum
Hardcover
240 pages
Jacket design by Muni Liebein
Value: $5-$8

Pope, Antoinette

One of the better-known founders of Chicago's rich and varied food culture, Antoinette Pope was the happy medium between home-style Betty Crocker and technical rock star Julia Child. A talented cook who learned the art of cookery from her in-laws, she and her husband Francois opened the Antoinette Pope School of Fancy Cookery in the basement of their south-side Chicago home in 1930.

The school flourished, and soon relocated to a more formal location on Michigan Ave., spawning the best-selling *Antoinette Pope School Cookbook* by 1948. The book went on to become yet another beloved culinary classic, with one documented anecdote telling of a woman who was buried with her copy (leaving her daughter to seek out a new copy for herself).

Antoinette and family wrote several other cookbooks over the years, including candy bible *The Antoinette Pope School's New Candy Cook Book*. The male Popes, father along with sons Frank and Robert, went on to host the popular local cooking show *Creative Cookery*, which was one of television's first cooking series. The school closed in the late 1970s.

1948
Antoinette Pope School Cookbook
Pope, Antoinette and Pope, Francois
MacMillan Co.
Hardcover
366 pages
Black-and-white photos
Value: $32-$56

1952
Cook's Quiz, A
Pope, Antoinette and Pope, Francois
Macmillan
Hardcover
188 pages
Value: $7-$12

Price, Mary and Vincent

Venerable film and television star Vincent Price along with his wife and Hollywood costume designer, Mary, were known within food circles as two of the most passionate and enthusiastic gourmets of their time. A pair of true food fanatics, they traveled the globe sampling fare from the finest restaurants and discussing food and techniques with a notable array of elite chefs and local home cooks.

In 1965, they released *A Treasury of Great Recipes*, an expansive volume of recipes from their travels. The book was a landmark publication, featuring never-before shared recipes, reprints of restaurant menus and glossy photos from the fabled kitchens of La Pyramide, Tre Scaline, the Ivy and the like—restaurants that most people would never even see, let alone dine at—all pressed between heavy metallic padded covers accented with silk bookmarks. In the 40 years since its release, the book has become one of the most beloved and sought-after of its kind.

With the help of historians and chefs, their subsequent cookbooks examined regional and historic American recipes.

1965
Treasury Of Great Recipes, A
Price, Mary and Price, Vincent
Ampersand Press
Hardcover
455-plus pages
First printing by Ampersand Press. Padded copper-colored cover with gold design
Designed by Arthur Hawkins, Illustrated by Fritz Kredel.
Recipes tested by Ann Seranne
Considered a landmark work
Value: $67-$119
Later editions command substantially less.

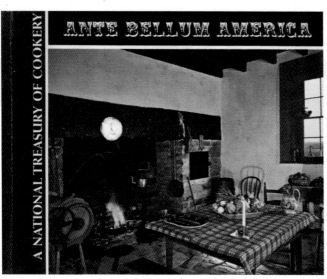

1967

National Treasury Of Cookery

Price, Mary and Vincent; Bullock, Helen Duprey
Heirloom Publishing
Hardcover
62 pages
Recipes of Ante Bellum America. Illustrations by Charles M. Wysocki. Compiled by Helen Duprey Bullock
Value: $11-$19

*Alternate
Cover*

1969

Come Into The Kitchen Cook Book

**Price, Mary; Price, Vincent; Bullock, Duprey Helen; Gaden, Eileen;
Misch, Robert Jay; Stein, Clem Jr.**
Stravon Educational Press
Hardcover
212 pages
Printed with several cover designs, but no difference in contents. Photos and drawings of antique utensils, foods and kitchens. Additional illustrations by Charles Wysocki and Nicholas Amorosi. Chapters and recipes by additional contributors
Value: $52-$93

Rawlings, Marjorie Kinnan

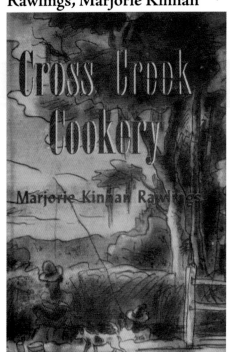

1942
Cross Creek Cookery
Rawlings, Marjorie Kinnan
Charles Scribner's and Sons
Hardcover
230 pages
Value: $39-$69

Rector, George

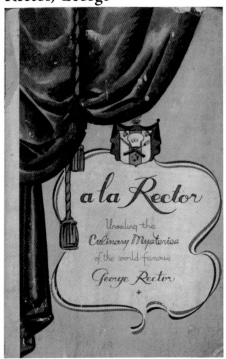

1933
A La Rector
Rector, George
Great Atlantic Pacific Tea Co.
Hardcover
111 pages
A delightful cookbook presented by Mr. Rector, owner of New York's Broadway restaurant of the same name. Witty writing and terrific period graphic design and illustrations (by Fred Breen) complement the anecdotes and recipes.
Spot color illustrations
Value: $21-$38

Robbins, Ann Roe

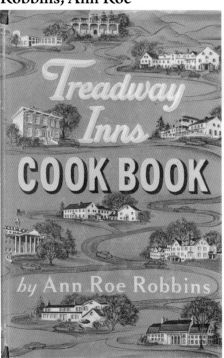

1958
Treadway Inns Cook Book
Robbins, Ann Roe
Little, Brown and Co.
Hardcover
397 pages
Recipes and history of the Treadway Inns. Each chapter begins with a drawing and description of a particular inn.
Value: $32-$56

Roberts, Ada Lou

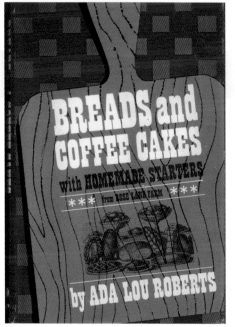

1967
Breads And Coffee Cakes With Homemade Starters From Rose Lane Farm
Roberts, Ada Lou
Hearthside Press
Hardcover
192 pages
Follow up to the popular *Favorite Breads from Rose Lane Farm*
Shown is the book club edition.
Value: $6-$11

Rombauer, Irma S.

Author of one of the most famous and significant cookbooks in American history, Irma S. Rombauer was an unlikely kitchen heroine. A privileged sophisticate in the early 1900s, she had little to no cooking experience when her husband committed suicide in 1930—making her decision to support herself by self-publishing a cookbook all the more ludicrous to friends and family.

The first edition of *The Joy of Cooking* (1931), compiled by Irma and illustrated by her daughter Marion (who later became her writing partner), was an unassuming recipe guide with a sweet, German-American slant. However, subsequent editions (over a half-dozen ranging from 1936 to 2006) made the book a national bestseller, largely due to the author's unique, breezy style and the relentless revisions, reorganizations and modern updates made by Irma, Marion and other professional contributors after the Rombauers' deaths.

As it evolved, the book became an almost encyclopedic guide to all things gourmet, explained in terms that the average home cook could understand. In 70 years, the book has never failed to stay relevant.

Irma wrote a dash of other cookbooks before her death in 1962, namely *Streamlined Cooking* (1939) and the successful children's cookery guide *A Cookbook for Girls and Boys* (1946).

Rombauer's *Joy of Cooking* is the only cookbook included in the 1995 New York Public Library's list of the 150 most influential books of the 20th century, taking its place beside Fitzgerald's *The Great Gatsby* and Einstein's *The Meaning of Relativity*.

1931
Joy Of Cooking
Rombauer, Irma S.
Bobbs-Merrill
Paperback
Few copies were printed of the first *Joy of Cooking*, and if found, may command prices upwards of $3,000.
1998 facsimile edition valued at $10-$20
Value: $2,100-$3,750

1936
Joy Of Cooking 1936
Rombauer, Irma S.
Bobbs-Merrill
Hardcover
628 pages
Value: $140-$250

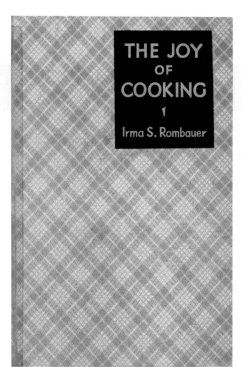

1941
Joy Of Cooking, The
Rombauer, Irma S.
Bobbs-Merrill Co.
Hardcover
628 pages
Illustrations by Marion Rombauer Becker
Shown: 6th printing, blue cover
Value: $39-$69

1941
Joy Of Cooking, The
Rombauer, Irma S.
Bobbs-Merrill Co.
Hardcover
628 pages
7th printing of 1941 edition with yellow cover
Value: $39-$69

1943
Joy Of Cooking
Rombauer, Irma S.
Bobbs-Merrill
Hardcover
1943 printing of the blue diamond cover—one of the most desirable editions. The 1946 printing with the same cover has slightly different contents.
Value: $55-$98

1946
Joy Of Cooking 1943 edition, 1946 printing
Rombauer, Irma S.
Bobbs-Merrill
Hardcover
884 pages
The 1943 edition with the blue diamond cover is one of the most desirable editions and was printed through 1946. However, while all printings with this cover have the same number of pages and essentially the same recipes, the 1943 wartime printing has extra chapters related to wartime cooking. Wartime editions fetch the higher value noted. Showing dust jacket.
Value: $41-$73

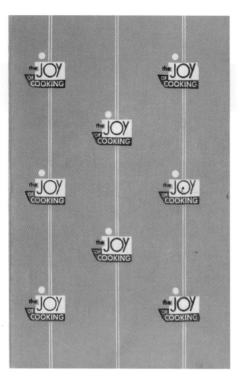

1953
Joy Of Cooking, The
Rombauer, Irma S. and Becker, Marion Rombauer
Bobbs-Merrill
Hardcover
1,013 pages
Illustrated by Ginnie Hofmann
Value: $30-$53

1962
Joy Of Cooking, The
Rombauer, Irma S. and Becker, Marion Rombauer
Bobbs-Merrill Co.
Hardcover
852 pages
Illustrations by Ginnie Hofmann and Beverly Warner. The first printing of the 1962 edition was printed without the help of Irma Rombauer and suffered from quite a few errors. Subsequent printings of this edition with the same cover corrected the errors.
Value: $30-$53

1962-1973
Joy Of Cooking, The
Rombauer, Irma S. and Becker, Marion Rombauer
Bobbs-Merrill
Hardcover
Revised and enlarged, over 4,300 recipes, 1,200 new recipes, new illustrations
Value: $29-$53

1975-1981
Joy Of Cooking
Rombauer Becker, Marion
Bobbs-Merrill Co.
Hardcover
915 pages
White washable cover with gold lettering. Showing the dust jacket.
Value: $30-$53

Rorer, Sarah Tyson

For a woman who originally had no interest in cooking or domestic life (she was more interested in science), Sarah Tyson Rorer became one of the most significant food experts of her time. An editor, author and one of the country's first practicing dietitians, Mrs. Rorer was a champion of vegetables, hygiene and healthy eating.

Her love of chemistry and medicine led to a career in nutrition, where she would have happily stayed had friends not lured her into teaching in 1879. Shortly thereafter, Mrs. Rorer founded the Philadelphia Cooking School, and went on to lecture about dietetics, domestic science, cookery and common sense. "We eat 10 times more than we need," she once told an audience in the course of doing public tours and appearing on radio shows. During this time she became something of a food celebrity and spoke at venues such as NYC's Madison Square Garden.

Mrs. Rorer authored over 25 books during her career, including her exhaustive masterwork *Mrs. Rorer's New Cook Book: A Manual of Housekeeping* (1902), which contained over 1,500 recipes and helpful hints. Her books preached the value of fresh produce in the diet and contained meal plans featuring nutrient-rich recipes. She also penned *Mrs. Rorer's Diet for the Sick: Dietetic Treatment of Diseases of the Body ... ,* perhaps the first mainstream, food-based "alternative" medicine guide published for modern consumers.

See also: Recipe Booklets: Snowdrift, Rumford.

Additional Titles

Bread and Bread Making
Cakes, Cake Decorations and Desserts
Home Candy Making
Hot Weather Dishes
Household Accounts
How to Use a Chafing Dish
Made Over Dishes
Mrs. Rorer's Cakes, Icings and Fillings
Mrs. Rorer's Dainties
Mrs. Rorer's Diet for the Sick
Mrs. Rorer's Every Day Menu Cook Book
Mrs. Rorer's Many Ways for Cooking Eggs
Mrs. Rorer's My Best 250 Recipes
New Ways for Oysters
Quick Soups
Sandwiches

1886
Mrs. Rorer's Philadelphia Cook Book
Rorer, Sarah Tyson
Arnold and Co.
Hardcover
581 pages plus ads
First edition
20 pages of advertisements at end of book
Value: $60-$106

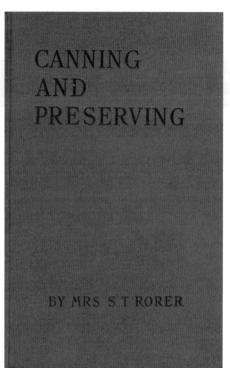

1887
Canning And Preserving
Rorer, Mrs. S.T.
Arnold & Co.
Hardcover
78 pages
Value: $55-$98

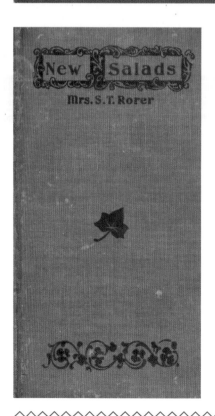

1897
New Salads
Rorer, Mrs. S.T.
Arnold and Co.
Hardcover
63 pages
Value: $32-$56

1902
Mrs. Rorer's New Cook Book
Rorer, Sarah Tyson
Arnold and Co.
Hardcover
731 pages plus several describing Rorer's cook books
Value: $39-$106

1914
Dainty Dishes For All The Year Round
Rorer, Mrs. S. T.
North Brothers Mfg.
Stapled booklet
64 pages
Extensive directions for using a rotary crank freezer
Black-and-white photos of mother and daughter making ice cream
Value: $25-$44

Rosen, Ruth Chier

Rosen, who wrote for leading national magazines on specialized food subjects, and her publisher husband produced many small gift-style cookbooks, most with appealing graphic design. Look for copies in excellent condition with their original boxes. Cocktail collectors should also look for the scarce *Guide to Pink Elephant Napkins*.

Additional titles
Ancestral Recipes of Shen Mei Lon
Cyrano De Casserole
Dig That Dish
From Nets to You
Have Cook Book Will Mary
His
Just Between Us
Nippon These
Pardon My Foie Gras
Pop. Monsieur
Restaurant-Tour
Spicemanship
Stirring Sauce-ery
Thank You, Mr. Columbus
The Balabusta's Best
The Big Spread
The Chefs' Tour
The Epicurean Guide
The Spirit of Cooking
The Terrace Chef
Wendy's Kitchen Debut
Wick and Lick
Wurst You Were Here

1951, 1957
Guide To Pink Elephants, A
Rosen, Ruth Chier
Rosen
Sotcover, plastic comb binding
196 pages
Difficult to find in any condition. Has added cross-collector appeal for "Pink Elephant" collectors and cocktail book collectors
Volume 1 dated 1951. Volume 2 dated 1957. Tab-indexed with illustrations showing appropriate drink glass for each drink
Value: $53-$94

1953
Tomato Well Dressed, A: The Art Of Salad Making
Rosen, Ruth Chier
Richards Rosen
Soft cover, plastic comb binding
144 pages
Value: $9-$16

1955
Tooth Sweet
Rosen, Ruth Chier
Rosen
Soft cover, plastic comb binding
140 pages
Available in two cover designs. Price shown for book with original box.
Value: $31-$56

Circa 1955
Gourmet's Guide
Rosen, Ruth Chier
Rosen
Soft cover, plastic comb binding
194 pages
Undated circa 1955. Plastic-coated, index-style recipe cards
Value: $6-$11

1960
Freeze N' Easy
Rosen, Ruth Chier
Richards Rosen
Soft cover, plastic comb binding
140 pages
Value: $12-$21

1960
State Fair Blue Ribbon Preserving And Pickling Recipes
Rosen, Ruth Chier
Richards Rosen
Soft cover, plastic comb binding
140 pages
Black-and-white photos and illustrations. Tab indexed
Value: $11-$19

Savarin

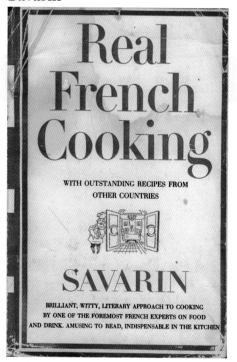

1956
Real French Cooking
Savarin
Doubleday & Co.
Hardcover
399 pages
Translated from the French
Value: $12-$21

Seranne, Ann

Best known for her wonderful cookbooks and time as an editor at *Gourmet* magazine, Ann Seranne was a food consultant, book author and food writer. Loved by the average homemaker and extravagant food fanatics alike, Ann's understanding of good food and how it should be prepared led to a collection of over 20 cookbooks, all of which were laced with her well-explained recipes and food musings.

She was a personal favorite of former *New York Times* restaurant critic and food editor Craig Claiborne, who called her "a born cook." He was particularly fond of her desserts, which she made for him personally on more than one occasion.

Several Junior League cookbooks as well as the masterpiece *America Cooks*, a General Federation of Women's Clubs fundraiser, owe their success to savvy editing by Seranne.

1949
Art Of Egg Cookery, The
Seranne, Anne
Doubleday & Co.
Hardcover
192 pages
Jacket design by Ben Feder
Value: $23-$43

1964
Sandwich Book, The
Seranne, Ann
Doubleday
Hardcover
151 pages
Value: $12-$22

1966
Complete Book Of Home Freezing, The
Seranne, Ann
Doubleday
Hardcover
350 pages
Value: $6-$11

Shircliffe, Arnold

Caterer for the famous and elegant Chicago Edgewater Beach Hotel, his menu collection is now housed as part of the New York Public Library ephemera collection.

Also look for the 1930s version of the *The Edgewater Sandwich and Hors D'oeuvres Book*.

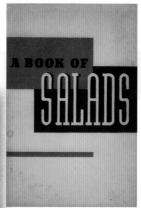

1926, 1944, 1951
Edgewater Beach Hotel Salad Book, The
Shircliffe, Arnold
Hotel Monthly Press
Hardcover
306 pages
Reprinted several times with various cover designs. 1951 cover shown
More than 800 salad and dressing recipes
Color photos
Value: $60-$106

Showalter, Mary Emma

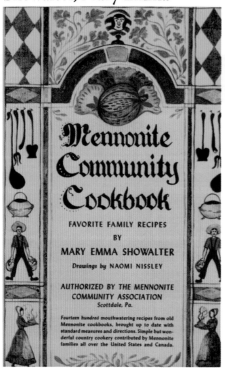

1950
Mennonite Community Cookbook
Showalter, Mary Emma
Holt, Rhinehart and Winston
Hardcover
494 pages
Drawings by Naomi Nissley. Color and black and white photos and illustrations
Reprinted in the 1990s. Earlier printings indicate 1,400 recipes and later printings indicate 1,100 recipes, but all editions have same number of pages.
1950 dust jacket has pictures of author and illustrator.
Value: $46-$81

Sidon, Alice

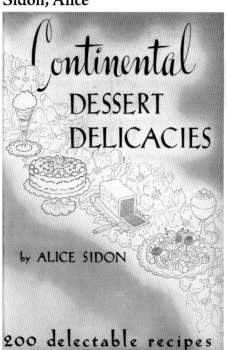

1950
Continental Dessert Delicacies
Sidon, Alice
M. Barrows & Co.
Hardcover
186 pages
Value: $16-$28

Simmons, Amelia

Author of what is generally considered the first truly American cookbook. While there are several appealing reprints, notably a 1960s version by Applewood Books, the original 1796 printing is very rare.

1984
The First American Cookbook Facismile Of American Cookery, 1796
Simmons, Amelia
Dover
Soft cover
Value: $7-$12

Simon, André

Agourmet, wine connoisseur, historian and admired bibliophile, André Simon was a man known for his exquisite taste and matching passion for food. A Parisian by birth, he was once quoted as saying, "A man dies too young if he leaves any wine in his cellar."

He was aptly lured to England by champagne, signing on as an agent for respected bubbly producers Pommery and Greno. André's work for the company led to his first book, a trade publication titled *The History of the Champagne Trade in England* (1905). It was not a commercial success. However, his passion for writing and expansive culinary knowledge soon led to several other trade publications, all of which paved the way for his commercially received *Wine and Spirits: The Connoisseur's Textbook* (1919).

Praised for his contagious love of food and clean, clear writing style, André went on to publish well over a dozen books on wine and food, including *The Art of Good Living* (1929) and *A Concise Encyclopedia of Gastronomy* (1952). He also founded the celebrated Wine and Food Society, which, in combination with a quarterly magazine appropriately titled *Wine and Food*, edited by André, helped to reform fine gastronomy and food in England before, during and even after World War II. The society still exists today under the name The International Wine and Food Society.

1948
André Simon's French Cook Book
Simon, André (edited by Crosby Gaige)
Little, Brown and Co.
Hardcover
342 pages
Value: $12-$21

Splint, Sarah Field

1930
Art Of Cooking And Serving, The
Splint, Sarah Field
Procter & Gamble
Hardcover
252 pages
Promotional cookbook for Proctor & Gamble and Crisco
Color and black-and-white photos throughout include those
of the properly dressed maid, tea service, kitchen utensils
and finished recipes.
Copyright dates vary, but contents are the same, 1930-
1936.
Value: $12-$21

Stoker, Catharine Ulmer

1946
Concha's Mexican Kitchen Cook Book
Stoker, Catharine Ulmer
The Naylor Co.
Hardcover
244 pages
Stories, customs, recipes and holidays. Records special
foods for occasions including weddings, Christmas, New
Years, Lent, Easter and birthdays, as well as everyday
recipes for all parts of the meal.
Spanish and English recipe names given
Value: $34-$61

Sunset

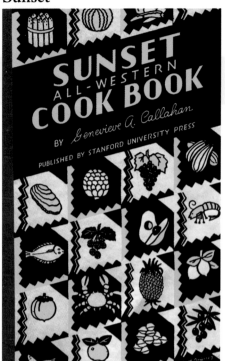

1933
Sunset All-Western Cook Book
Callahan, Genevieve A.
Stanford University Press
Soft cover
216 pages
Value: $32-$56

1933
Sunset's Favorite Company Dinners
Sunset
Lane Publishing
Stapled booklet
79 pages
Black-and-white illustrations
Value: $4-$7

1937
Sunset's Hostess Handbook
Sunset
Lane Publishing
Stapled booklet
96 pages
Value: $23-$41

1938
Sunset's New Kitchen Cabinet Cook Book
Sunset
Sunset Magazine
Soft cover, wire bound
224 pages
All of the recipes from the *Sunset Magazine* "Kitchen Cabinet" column published over a 10-year period, from February 1929 to June 1938
Highly illustrated with step-by-step black-and-white 1930s drawings
Recipes are attributed to contributors by initials, city and state.
Value: $18-$31

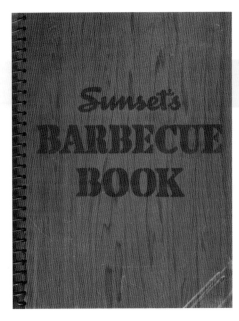

1938, 1939
Sunset's Barbecue Book
Sanderson, George and Rich, Virginia
Sunset
Hardcover, wood
72 pages
Likely the first book ever published on the subject of home barbecuing. Includes plans for barbecue building and recipes The original edition has an actual wood cover. Later printings are faux printed to look like wood.
Value: $49-$88

COLLECTING TIP
The acidic wood cover of the 1938 *Sunset Barbecue Book* wreaks havoc on first and last pages, making them brittle and discolored. Insert acid neutral paper between these to help minimize further damage.

1939
Sunset's Dessert Book
Editors of *Sunset*
Sunset Magazine
Soft cover
Value: $5-$9

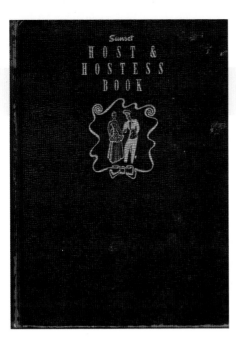

1940-1945
Sunset Host & Hostess Book
Muhs, Helen Kroeger (editor)
Lane Publishing
Hardcover
180 pages
Illustrations by Phyllis Gregg
Value: $27-$48

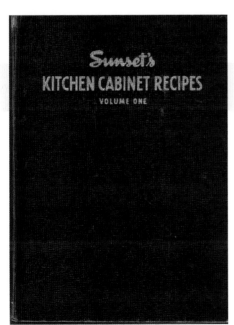

1940s
Sunset's Kitchen Cabinet Recipes
Volumes 1, 2 And 3
Editors of *Sunset*
Lane Publishing
Hardcover
Recipes contributed by readers to *Sunset Magazine's*
"Kitchen Cabinet" column, from 1929 through 1943, and
then reprinted in three volumes. Volume 1 covers recipes
originally printed from 1929-1933.
Price shown for each volume in the series
Value: $20-$36

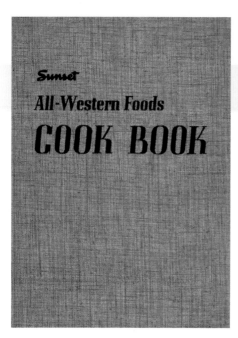

1947-1949
Sunset All-Western Foods Cook Book
Callahan, Genevieve A.
Lane
Hardcover
284 pages
Pictured are 1947 and 1949 editions, each with identical contents
Black and white illustrations
Value: $24-$43

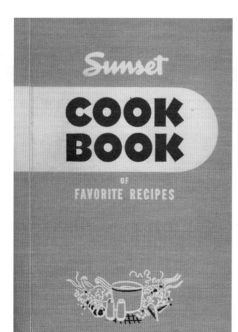

1949, 1952, 1957
Sunset Cook Book Of Favorite Recipes
Chase, Emily (editor)
Lane Publishing Co.
Hardcover, wire bound
415 pages
Finest recipes that appeared in *Sunset Magazine* over 20 years
Cover colors vary but contents identical
Shown is the 1949 green cover.
Value: $25-$44

1961
Sunset Cook Book Of Favorite Recipes
Chase, Emily (editor)
Lane
Paperback
415 pages
Same contents as 1949 edition
Value: $11-$19

1950
Sunset Barbecue Book
Editors of *Sunset*
Lane Publishing
Soft cover
96 pages
Third Edition. How to build and use barbecues
17 detailed plans, 275 illustrations. Many photos with mid-century examples
Value: $25-$44

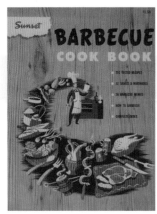

1950
Sunset Barbecue Cook Book
Editors of *Sunset*
Paperback
96 pages
251 recipes, 37 sauces and marinades, 26 menus, fire pit cooking and how to barbecue Spot color illustrations
Value: $12-$21

1957
Sunset Barbecue Cook Book
Editors of *Sunset*
Lane Publishing
Soft cover
192 pages
2nd edition. Direct descendent of original 1938 printing. Long considered one of the best guides to outdoor cooking Black-and-white photos. Spot color illustrations
Value: $21-$38

1957
Sunset Cooking Bold And Fearless
Editors of *Sunset*
Lane Book Co.
Hardcover
220 pages plus index
Recipes from the Chefs-of-the-West championship. Recipes attributed to contributors Illustrations by Harry O. Diamond.
Value: $20-$36

1957
Sunset Salad Book
Chase, Emily (editor)
Lane Publishing
Soft cover
90 pages plus index
Originally printed in 1946. Pictured is the 1947 vinyl, washable cover.
Black-and-white photos and illustrations
Value: $11-$19

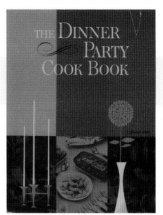

1960
Sunset Cook Book, The
Editors of *Sunset*
Lane Book Co.
Hardcover
216 pages
Illustrated by Earl Thollander
Value: $10-$19

1962
Dinner Party Cook Book, The
Sunset Editorial Staff
Lane Book Co.
Hardcover
232 pages
Designed and illustrated by William S. Shields
Color and black-and-white photos and illustrations
Value: $11-$19

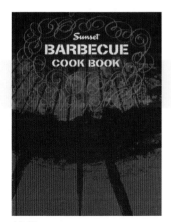

1962
Sunset Barbecue Cook Book
Editors of *Sunset*
Lane Publishing
Hardcover
160 pages
Part of a gift set with slipcase, and originally paired with the
Sunset Salad Book. Design by Adrian Wilson. Illustrations
by William Shields. Black-and-white photos and spot color
illustrations
Value: $14-$25
Set with slipcase: $40-$45

1962
Sunset Salad Book
Editors of *Sunset*
Lane Publishing
Hardcover
160 pages
Part of a gift set with slipcase, and originally paired with
the *Sunset Barbecue Book.* Design by Adrian Wilson.
Illustrations by Earl Thollander. Black-and-white photos and
spot color illustrations
Value: $7-$13
Set with slipcase: $40-$45

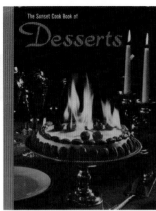

1963

Sunset Cook Book Of Desserts, The

Editors of *Sunset*
Lane
Hardcover
125 pages plus index
Sunset cookbook with unusual dessert recipes like "Apple Pannukakku," "Chocolate Pancake Tower" and "Arab Pumpkin Pudding"
Black-and-white photos
Value: $13-$23

1964

Sunset Adventures In Food

Editors of *Sunset*
Lane Publishing
Hardcover
192 pages
Color illustrations by Alice Harth
Value: $9-$16

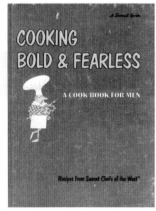

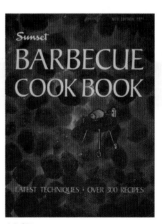

1967

Cooking Bold And Fearless

Editors of *Sunset*
Lane Publishing Co.
Hardcover
160 pages
Value: $13-$23

1967

Sunset Barbecue Cook Book

Editors of *Sunset*
Lane
Soft cover
160 pages
Spot color illustrations and black-and-white photos
Illustrations by Carol Johnston
Value: $11-$19

Supermother

1969-1971

Supermother's Cooking With Grass Gourmet Recipe Cards

Supermother
Ravenshurst Pleasure Product
Stapled booklet or separate cards
15 pages
Subtitled "Recipe Cards featuring the Cannibal's Canapes (Cooked Cock Recipe)" Envelope with 15 separate recipe cards using marijuana as an ingredient. Recipe examples: Shrimp Creole, Date Nut Bars, Pot Tea ...
Undated circa 1969
Shown: booklet version with head shop paraphernalia ad on inside back cover
Value: $32-$56

Times-Picayune

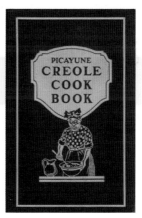

1954

Original Picayune Creole Cook Book, The

Times-Picayune
Hardcover
438 pages
Reprinted many times, with first edition printed in 1900 or 1901. Each edition is slightly different and collectible in its own right. The 12th edition, a 1954 printing, is shown. Frontispiece has color drawing of African-American cook in a Creole kitchen circa 1875.
Value: $32-$56

1901
Dining Room And Kitchen
Townsend, Grace
Home Publishing Co.
Hardcover
527 pages
Revised edition of *Dining Room and Kitchen,* an economical guide in "Practical Housekeeping for the American Housewife containing the Choicest Tried and Approved Cookery Recipes"
Black-and-white engravings
Value: $123-$219

Tracy, Marian

The day after the Japanese bombed Pearl Harbor, Marian Tracy's first edition of *Casserole Cookery* appeared in bookstores. World War II food rationing compelled the nation's cooks to scrimp, save and rethink the American menu, and so, though Marian couldn't have predicted it, her cookbook was propelled into American cooking history.

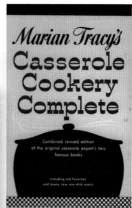

1956
Marian Tracy's Casserole Cookery Complete
Tracy, Marian
Viking
Hardcover, wire bound
Wire-bound, flip-top, lay-flat binding. Combined, revised edition of the original casserole expert's two famous books
Value: $16-$28

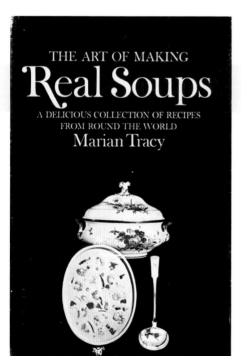

1967
Art Of Making Real Soups, The
Tracy, Marian
Doubleday
Hardcover
249 pages
Value: $11-$19

Trader Vic

Trader Vic

Trader Vic (Victor Bergeron) was the owner and creator of "Trader Vic's Trading Post" Tiki Bar and restaurant (originally named "Hinky Dink's"), in Oakland, Calif. He is often credited as the creator of the Mai Tai cocktail, although Don the Beachcomber vies for the title as well. Their two recipes for this now famous cocktail bear little resemblance to each other and the debate rages on.

1947, 1948
Bartender's Guide ... By Trader Vic
Trader Vic
Doubleday
Hardcover
437 pages
Cocktail guide with over 1,500 recipes for home and professional bartender. Humorous, conversational style
Illustrated by Ray Sullivan
Value: $52-$93

1946
Trader Vic's Book Of Food & Drink
Trader Vic
Doubleday
Hardcover
Showing 1946 dust jacket and cover. Later printings (1980s) have black-and-white reproductions of original color drawings and command only $5-$15.
Value: $34-$60

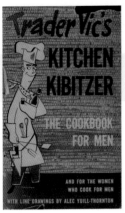

1952
Trader Vic's Kitchen Kibitzer
Trader Vic
Doubleday
Hardcover
223 pages
Line drawings by Alec Yuill-Thronton
Value: $12-$22

1968
Trader Vic's Pacific Island Cookbook
Trader Vic
Doubleday
Hardcover
287 pages
Value: $20-$36

Tyree, Marion Cabell

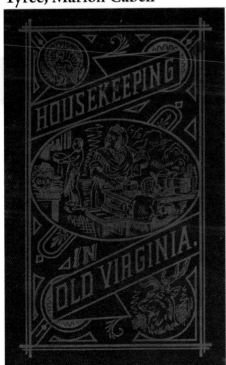

1879, 1965
Housekeeping In Old Virginia
Tyree, Marion Cabell
John P. Morton
Hardcover
528 pages
Showing facsimile Favorite Recipes Press reprint of the classic 1879 cookbook
Contributions from 250 of Virginia's noted housewives, distinguished for their skill in the culinary art and other branches of domestic economy
Recipes attributed to contributors
Value: $12-$22

Vaughn, Kate Brew

An enthusiastic promoter of the household arts, Kate Brew Vaughn was considered an expert on all things kitchen and home during the first half of the 1900s. A California-based dietitian, journalist and mother of five, her tips and reflections on home economics in the modern world appeared in publications such as *The Los Angeles Herald*, *The Los Angeles Evening Express Daily* and *The Journal of Home Economics*.

She was best known during her career for her popular national tours, during which she hosted talks and demonstrations on cooking and nutrition. She also made public appearances at local homemaking events and broadcasted for KNX Radio Los Angeles.

Though Kate published only a few titles during her career, her books remain hot commodities within the historic cookbook circles, most notably *Culinary Echoes from Dixie* (1914) and *My Best Recipes* (1929). The later is particularly unique in that Kate allowed companies whose products she approved to advertise within her pages, furthering the era's budding relationship between food companies and culinary personalities.

Also look for:

Up-to-the-Minute Cook Book
Art of Preserving and Canning
Table Treats for Wartime

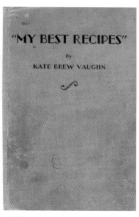

1914
Culinary Echoes From Dixie
Vaughn, Kate Brew
MacDonald Press
Hardcover
270-plus pages
Value: $70-$125

1929
My Best Recipes
Vaughn, Kate Brew
Hardcover
334 pages
Early cookbook by Kate Brew Vaughn of KNX Los Angeles Radio Station and a columnist for the *Los Angeles Evening Express Daily Newspaper*. Includes a photo of the author and advertisements by Carnation, Kellogg's, Pyrex, Ben-Hur Spices, Tea and Coffee, and Adohr Creamery.
Value: $46-$81

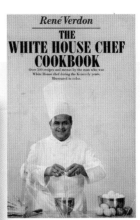

Verdon, René

In his youth, René learned the basics of his craft as a chef's helper in France (where allowing a dish to burn earned him a slap, kick or the chore of peeling a mountain of potatoes). He immigrated to the United States, finding work at the New York Essex House, where his talents were not overlooked and he was serendipitously recommended to the Kennedys as a chef for their son. He spent five memorable years as the White House chef, and he named one of his dishes "Clam Jacqueline" after Jackie Kennedy.

1968
White House Chef Cookbook, The
Verdon, René
Doubleday
Hardcover
287 pages
Recipes and anecdotes from the chef of the Kennedy administration
Value: $6-$11

Wakefield, Ruth

In 1930, Ruth Wakefield and her husband purchased the centuries-old Toll House Inn in Whitman, Mass., where Ruth, a former dietitian, served her signature homemade fare. An emergency substitute of crumbled chocolate bars in Ruth's chocolate cookie recipe, and culinary history was made.

Rumor has it she was not thrilled with the results of her substitution as she intended the chocolate to melt. Her employees, however, loved the chewy, chocolaty effect and one of the most treasured American treats—The Toll House Cookie (originally named "Toll House Crunch Cookies")—was born.

Dust Jacket

1945
Ruth Wakefield's Tried and True Recipes
Wakefield, Ruth
M. Barrows & Co.
Hardcover
Value: $28-$45

Waldo, Myra

Myra Waldo (Myra Waldo Schwartz) was a jet-setting food writer, editor and critic of enviable skill and beauty. A wordsmith with a passion for faraway places and native cuisine, she was educated at Columbia University before settling in as a journalist and author in the late 1950s and '60s.

Once labeled "the most traveled woman in the world" by the former president of the Society of American Travel Writers, Myra journeyed to every continent but Antarctica at a time when many women still lived their whole lives in the same state, and wrote over two dozen travel and food guides during her career. A member of the Screen Actors Guild, she was also seen and heard during numerous television appearances and on the radio as New York's WCBS News Radio 88 travel editor.

Like many food experts before her, Myra cooked for crowds and gave public demonstrations of techniques. Her cookbooks often featured cuisine from destinations like Africa, France and the Mediterranean.

Over 40 cookbooks to her name, most have some collectible interest.

Also look for:

1954: *Serve at Once: The Soufflé Cookbook*
1967: *The Dictionary of International Food and Cooking Terms*

1957
Slenderella Cook Book, The
Waldo, Myra
Putnam's
Hardcover
335 pages
Value: $14-$25

1001 WAYS TO PLEASE A HUSBAND

Myra Waldo

**The cookbook that makes you a success from the start—
quick and easy recipes for two (or more)—menus for
every season, every occasion—a wealth of kitchen
wisdom: planning, marketing, wines, freezing.**

1958
1,001 Ways To Please A Husband
Waldo, Myra
Van Nostrand
Hardcover
Value: $53-$94

1958
Beer And Good Food
Waldo, Myra
Doubleday
Hardcover
264 pages
Recipes and cocktails made with beer and ale. Includes beer
history. Color photos
Value: $6-$11

1962-1970
Cakes, Cookies And Pastries
Waldo, Myra
Galahad Books
Hardcover
125 pages
Value: $7-$12

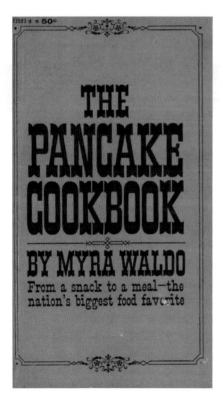

1963
Pancake Cookbook, The
Myra Waldo
Bantam
Paperback
146 pages
Value: $5-$8

Wallace, Lily Haxworth

A cookbook author, magazine writer, cookery teacher and kitchen enthusiast, Britain's Lily Haxworth Wallace did more for food in the 1900s than just write about it. As national president of the Associated Clubs of Domestic Science, Lily championed the "pure food" cause, calling for food reform and tougher labeling legislation (before the cause eventually won Congress over, you could put pretty much anything in a can and not admit to it).

A graduate of London's National Training School of Cookery, she went on to write over two dozen cookbooks, including *The Lily Wallace New American Cook Book* (1946); *Soups, Stews, and Chowders* (1945); and *The Rumford Complete Cookbook* (1908). The latter helped establish her as one of the era's most respected culinary experts, was an expansive cookery guide covering everything from braised beef to buckwheat pancakes, and still contains hundreds of recipes that are hearty by nature but frugal by design—one of Mrs. Wallace's specialties.

See also: Recipe Booklets: Rumford.

1912
Modern Cook Book And Household Recipes, The
Wallace, Lily Haxworth
Warner Library
Hardcover
1,127 pages
Value: $53-$94

1925
Rumford Complete Cook Book
Wallace, Lily Haxworth
The Rumford Co.
Hardcover
241 pages
Cover designs vary slightly over the life of the many reprints. Advertisement in the *Rumford Common Sense Cook Book* states that this cookbook will be mailed free for 12 cards from the 12-ounce cans of Rumford Baking Powder.
Value: $20-$36

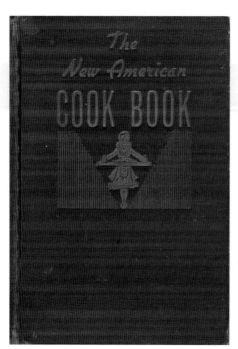

1941-44
New American Cook Book, The
Wallace, Lily Haxworth
American Publishers
Hardcover
932 pages
Cover colors vary but contents are identical
1941-1944
Thumb-indexed. Color and black-and-white photos and illustrations
Value: $49-$87

1945
Soups, Stews And Chowders
Wallace, Lily Haxworth
M. Barrows & Co.
Hardcover
242 pages
Value: $20-$36

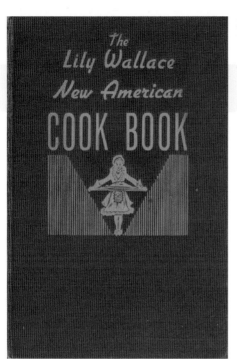

1946

Lily Wallace New American Cook Book, The

Wallace, Lily Haxworth
Books, Inc.
Hardcover
931 pages
Cover colors vary but contents are identical. Sequel to the 1941 edition. Color and black-and-white photos and illustrations
Value: $41-$73

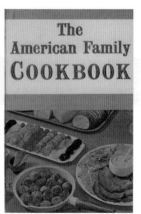

1950, 1954, 1963

American Family Cook Book, The

Wallace, Lily Haxworth
Books, Inc.
Hardcover
831 pages
Reprint of *The Lily Wallace New American Cook Book.* Paper in these editions tends to be very brittle and brown. Pictured are the dust jacket of 1950s printing and the glossy pictorial cover of 1960s printing. Contents are identical for these years.
Value: $28-$49

Walt Disney

1975
Walt Disney's Mickey Mouse Cookbook
Walt Disney
Golden Press
Hardcover
93 pages
Hard and soft cover available
Value: $34-$61

Welch, Mary Scott

1948
Your First Hundred Meals
Welch, Mary Scott
Charles Scribners
Hardcover, plastic comb binding
200 pages
Every meal complete with minute-by-minute instructions all on one page. Interior plastic comb binding
Value: $34-$60

White, Marion

1943
Diet Without Despair
White, Marion
M. S. Mill Co.
Hardcover
118 pages
By the author of *Sweets Without Sugar*
Value: $5-$9

William Wise Publishers

1948, 1949, 1951
Wise Encyclopedia Of Cookery, The
William Wise Publishers
William H. Wise & Co.
Hardcover
1,300-plus pages. Shown in scarce dust jacket.
Value: $30-$53

Woman's Day

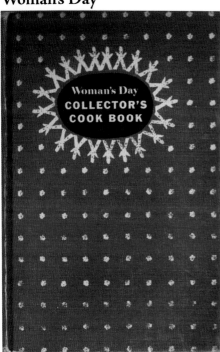

1960
Woman's Day Collector's Cook Book
Woman's Day
E. P. Dutton
Hardcover
320 pages
Illustrations by Joseph Low. Chapter introductions by James Beard. Reprinted many times in different sizes and covers
Value: $12-$21

1965, 1966, 1967
Woman's Day Encyclopedia Of Cookery
Editors of *Woman's Day*
Fawcett
Hardcover
Set of 12. Individual volumes range in price from $7-$25. Sets available from $125-$185
Value: $7-$25

1966
Woman's Day Cookie Cook Book
Author not noted
Fawcett
Soft cover
112 pages
Abridged edition
Value: $11-$19

1977
Woman's Day Book Of Baking
Harris, Diane (editor)
Simon & Schuster
Hardcover
320 pages
Value: $20-$36

Zelayeta, Elena

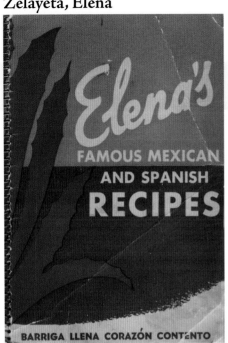

1944-1950s
Elena's Famous Mexican And Spanish Recipes
Zelayeta, Elena
Soft cover, wire bound
127 pages
Noted cook, lecturer and restaurateur, Elena Zelayeta shares her recipes for great Mexican food.
Illustrations by Philip Little and Norman Gordon
Value: $32-$56

DEFINITION

Letterpress: type of printing where raised metal type is pressed into the paper leaving slightly embossed impressions.

Elena's Fiesta Recipes
Zelayeta, Elena
Ward Ritchie Press
Hardcover
106 pages
Original hardcover letterpress printing shown. Later soft cover was revised and is valued at $15-$25.
Value: $32-$56

1958-1965
Elena's Secrets Of Mexican Cooking
Zelayeta, Elena
Prentice Hall
Hardcover
266 pages
Hundreds of traditional Mexican dishes, most with information about their history and use in Mexican or Mexican-American culture
Hardcover and paperback versions are pictured.
Value: $23-$41

1967
Elena's Favorite Foods California Style
Zelayeta, Elena
Prentice Hall
Hardcover
310 pages
Value: $10-$18

Chapter 2:
Charity Cookbooks

Charity cookbooks are commonly referred to as fundraiser or community cookbooks, or as "spirals." Regardless of what they are called, charity cookbooks are collections of recipes that have been published in America as fundraisers, for over 140 years, by churches, schools, service groups and other fraternal and cultural organizations.

While there are many commercially successful cookbooks that began as fundraisers, like *The Settlement Cookbook* and *Junior League* cookbooks, there are many more that were published in very small quantities or that were created by the hands of volunteers themselves, using whatever methods and resources they could muster (typewriters, mimeographs and copiers).

Cover and interior art is sometimes commercial clip-art, but the more endearing examples feature the artistic expressions of inspired volunteers, as is the case with the charity cookbook *Like Mama Used to Make*. There are many qualities that make a fundraiser cookbook desirable, not the least of which is the preservation of regional recipes. Also, look for books that are older (pre-1940s) and feature:

◆ Local advertisements

◆ Contributors noted by name

◆ Anecdotes or historical information

◆ Photos of local buildings

◆ Handwritten recipes

◆ Contributions by celebrities

◆ Unusual or interesting bindings

◆ Or those that are handmade or have exceptional illustrations

The category of charity cookbooks offers a special appeal for collectors, telling the personal stories of different eras, cultures, regions and the people who contributed to them. As you read through the recipes, essays, poems and anecdotes, you get to know the communities and the period in which these books were created.

Further Reading:

◆ *Culinary Americana*, Eleanor and Bob Brown, 1961

◆ *Sweets and Meats Early Texas Cookbooks*, 1855-1936 and reprinted in 2005, Elizabeth Borst White

◆ Ask your local librarian if there is a specific bibliography of cookbooks available that covers your region or area of interest.

Alabama, Spring Hill

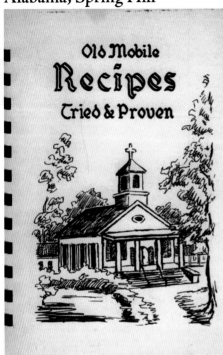

1956
Old Mobile Recipes Tried & Proven
St. Margaret's Guild of St. Paul's Episcopal Church
Soft cover, plastic comb binding
100 pages
Recipes attributed to contributors
Value: $28-$49

Alaska, Fairbanks

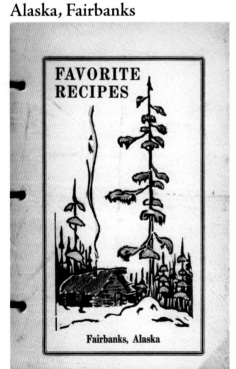

1944
Favorite Recipes Fairbanks, Alaska
Saint Matthew's Guild
Saint Matthew's Episcopal Church
Soft cover
160 pages
Hand colored cover. Local ads. Recipes attributed to contributors
Value: $48-$86

Arizona, Tucson

1960
Favorite Recipes Tucson First Ward
Tucson, Arizona
Tucson First Ward Primary
Soft cover, plastic comb binding
229 pages
Recipes attributed to contributors
Value: $7-$13

California, Burlingame

1951
Lincoln Gourmet Burlingame,
California
Lincoln P.T.A.
Soft cover
40 pages
Recipes attributed to contributors
Value: $14-$25

California, National City

1925
Tested Recipes C. H. M. Class Baptist Church National City, Calif.
C. H. M. Class Baptist Church National City, Calif.
Soft cover
75 pages
Recipes attributed to contributors
Value: $34-$61

California, Oakland

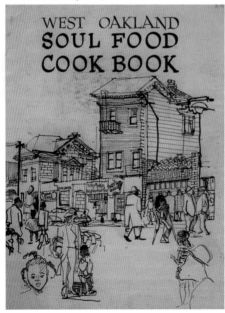

Circa 1966
West Oakland Soul Food Cook Book
Peter Maurin Neighborhood House
Stapled booklet
47 pages
Undated circa 1966
Exceptional drawings by John Baldwin throughout
Handwritten and contains a wealth of soul food recipes like
Mrs. Ruby Hanton's Hog's Head Stew and Mrs. Beatrice
Hall's Blackeyed Peas with Neckbones. Includes a few home
remedies
Value: $53-$94

California, San Francisco

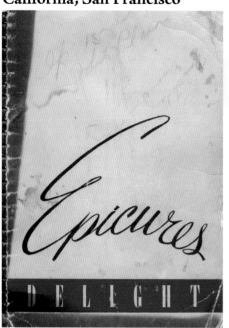

1944
Epicures Delight
British War Relief of San Francisco
Soft cover, wire bound
253 pages
Value: $27-$48

California, Santa Barbara

1928
Philathea Cook Book
Philathea Class
First Methodist Episcopal Church
Hardcover
199 pages
Class officers noted. Recipes attributed to contributors.
Local advertisements
Value: $38-$68

California, Sonoma County

1934
Loyalty Cook Book
Willow Borba Santa Rosa Parlor No. 217
Willow Borba
Soft cover
194 pages
Native Daughters of the Golden West charity cookbook,
second edition
Bound with binding tape (original). Recipes attributed to
contributors from around the state. Membership listing
Value: $59-$106

Connecticut, Five Mile River

1955
Five Mile River Cookbook
United Church of Rowayton, Conn.
Soft cover, plastic comb binding
176 pages
A collection of recipes by residents in the area of Five Mile
River, Conn., for the benefit of the building fund of the
United Church of Rowayton
Scarce
Black-and-white illustrations
Each recipe handwritten by contributor
Value: $102-$181

Connecticut, Manchester

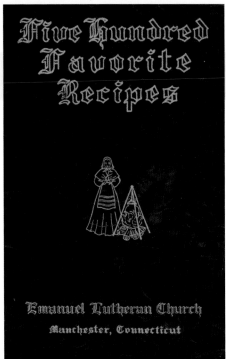

Circa 1940

Five Hundred Favorite Recipes

Dorcas Society

Emanuel Lutheran Church, Manchester, Conn.

Soft cover, plastic comb binding
150 pages
Fundraiser features recipes from the local residents and
church members of Manchester, Conn., circa 1940. Recipes
favor Swedish heritage like Swedish Brown Beans, Pottches,
Hotmos and Skorpor. Recipes attributed to contributors
Value: $44-$78

Connecticut, Westport

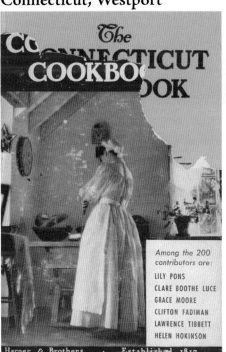

1944

Connecticut Cookbook, The

The Westport Woman's Club

Harper & Brothers
Hardcover
261 pages
Famous contributors and expert illustrations combined with
wartime sensibility
Value: $67-$119

Connecticut, Westport

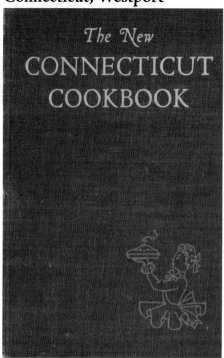

1947
New Connecticut Cookbook, The
The Westport Woman's Club
Harper & Brothers
Hardcover
338 pages
Revised version of the appealing Connecticut community cookbook by the Woman's Club of Westport with illustrations contributed by well-known Connecticut artists.
Contributors include Gladys Taber, Lousene Rousseau Fry and Clare Boothe Luce. Recipes attributed to contributors.
Black-and-white illustrations
Value: $67-$119

Delaware, Wilmington

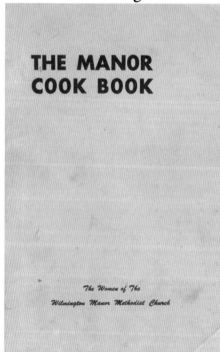

Circa 1935
Manor Cook Book, The
Women of Wilmington Manor Methodist Church
Soft cover
148 pages plus ads
A scarce Delaware fundraiser cookbook
Difficult to date—somewhere between 1920 and 1940
Many local advertisements. Recipes are attributed to contributors.
Value: $60-$106

Floria, Bradenton

1963
Mandy Lou's Kitchen Secrets
Harmony Helpers of the Universal Spiritualist Church
Bev-Ron
Soft cover, plastic comb binding
50-plus pages
Florida regional fundraiser charity cookbook by the Harmony Helpers of the Universal Spiritualist Church
Local advertisements. Recipes attributed to contributors, who hail from around the nation
Value: $27-$48

Illinois, Chicago

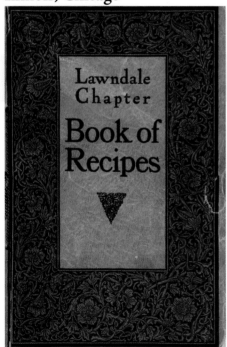

1931
Lawndale Chapter Book Of Recipes Chapter No. 749 Order Of Eastern Star
Lawndale Chapter of Illinois Easter Star
Lawndale Chicago
Soft cover
184 pages
7th Edition of the *Lawndale Chapter No. 749 Cookbook*
Attractive brown paper cover with hand-tassel binding
Recipes show names of contributors.
Value: $56-$100

Illinois, Chicago

1946
Thoughts For Food
Institute Publishing
Houghton Mifflin
Hardcover
372 pages
Institute Publishing is the pseudonym for a group of Chicago hostesses who assembled their combined culinary knowledge for civic charity.
A companion to *Thoughts for Buffets*
Value: $6-$11

Illinois, Chicago

1958
Thoughts For Buffets
Institute Publishing
Houghton Mifflin
Hardcover
425 pages
Companion to *Thoughts for Food*
Value: $12-$22

Illinois, Elgin

1948
Granddaughter's Inglenook Cookbook
Brethren Publishing
Brethren Publishing House
Hardcover
320 pages
Successor to the earlier *Inglenook Cookbook*
Value: $32-$56

Illinois, Elmhurst

1951
Cook Book
Elmhurst Methodist Church, Elmhurst, Ill.
Elmhurst Methodist Church Women's Society for Christian Service
Soft cover, plastic comb binding
146 pages
Sample recipes include: Bundy's Delight and Heavenly Hash Salad. Recipes attributed to contributors
Value: $25-$44

Indiana, Danville

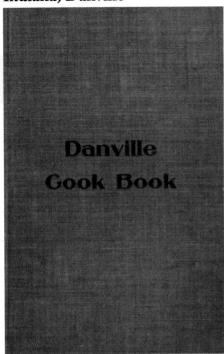

1897
Danville Cook Book
Ladies of the Christian Church, Danville, Indiana
Hardcover
163 pages plus ads
20 pages of local advertisements. Recipes attributed to contributors
Value: $102-$181

Kansas, Wichita

1944-1945
Greetings Cook Book 20th Century Club
20th Century Club
Hardcover
194 pages
Dedicated to brides who received it as a courtesy of the advertisers. Many local advertisements
Recipes attributed to contributors
First edition printed in 1929 and one printed in each subsequent year. Includes an illustration of the entrance to The Twentieth Century Club at Elm and Broadway, Wichita, Kansas.
Value: $39-$69

Maine

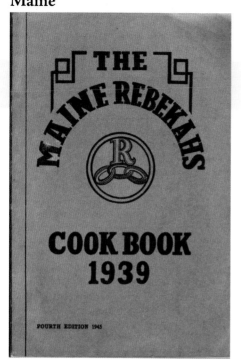

1939-1941
Maine Rebekahs Cook Book, The
Maine Rebekahs
Soft cover
Includes a listing of past Rebekah presidents and their slogans
Three editions: 1939, 1940 and 1941
Value: $46-$81

Maryland, St. Mary's County

1975
300 Years Of Black Cooking In St. Mary's County Maryland
Citizens for Progress
Paperback
131 pages
Maryland regional fundraiser charity cookbook by the Citizens for Progress celebrating the traditional foods of Black people. Recipes attributed to contributors. Handwritten recipes
Value: $53-$94

COLLECTING TIP

Handwritten (as opposed to typeset) recipe compilations have an added feeling of authenticity often enhancing the character and desirability of a book. These are more common and especially desirable in fundraiser cookbooks where the recipes are reproduced using the actual handwritten recipe supplied by the contributor.

Massachusetts, Haverhill

1882
Pentucket Housewife
Ladies of the First Baptist Church, Haverhill, Mass.
Hardcover
126-plus pages
Exceptional printing and local historic references distinguishes this early Massachusetts fundraising cookbook with ornate printer's embellishments at each chapter head. Advertisements are plentiful. Recipes attributed to contributors
Value: $840-$1,500

Michigan, Ann Arbor

1952
Like Mama Used To Make
Women of the Ann Arbor Chapter of Hadassah
Soft cover, plastic comb bound
196 pages
A collection of favorite and traditional Jewish dishes including Pumpernickel Pie, Kugels, Verenickes, Rogelach and Mandlen. Charming illustrations. Recipes attributed to contributors
Value: $39-$69

Minnesota, Nakomis Heights

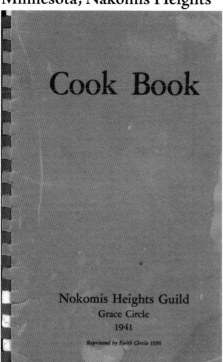

1941, 1956
Cook Book Nokomis Heights Guild Grace Circle
Nokomis Heights Guild
Soft cover, plastic comb bound
1956 reprint of the 1941 *Nokomis Heights Guild Grace Circle Fundraiser* cookbook
Scarce
Recipes attributed to contributors
Value: $28-$49

Missouri, St. Louis

1964
Saint Louis Cookbook, The
Rabenberg, Mrs. William (editor)
Women's Association of the St. Louis Symphony Society
Soft cover, comb bound
308 pages
Bicentennial issue
Recipes attributed to contributors
Peppered with St. Louis culinary trivia. Drawings and photos of local buildings with architects identified
Value: $32-$56

Nebraska, Davenport

1937
Davenport Community Cook Book
Davenport Woman's Club, Davenport, Nebraska
Soft cover, wire bound
191 pages
Recipes attributed to contributors. Local and national advertisements
Value: $66-$119

Nebraska, Omaha

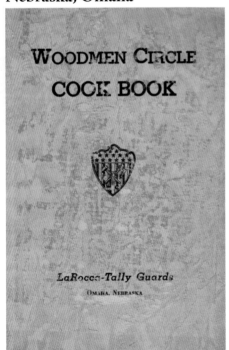

1930s
Woodmen Circle Cook Book
Omaha, Nebraska Aksarben
Larocca-Talley Guards
Soft cover
136 pages
Value: $66-$118

Nevada, Lamoille

1954
50th Anniversary Recipe Roundup
Lamoille, Nevada Mizpah Society
Mizpah Society of the Lamoille
Presbyterian Church
Paperback
56 pages
One historic church photo and some church history. Recipes
attributed to contributors
Value: $21-$38

Nevada, Reno

1924
Good Things To Eat
Women of Trinity Guild
Stapled booklet
190 pages
Local advertisements
Value: $59-$106

Nevada, Reno

1928
Nevada Vocational Home Economics Tested Recipes
Vocational Home Economics Classes of Nevada
Stapled booklet
Early regional cookbook by the Vocational Home Economics Classes of Nevada
Title page shows photo of Virginia Valley High School girls in the home economics laboratory. Includes early advertising for Sparks, Reno, Battle Mountain and Carson City businesses
Scarce
Recipes attributed to contributors.
Value: $88-$156

Nevada, Winnemucca

1914
Cook Book Ladies' Aid Society Of The First Methodist Episcopal Church
Ladies' Aid Society First Methodist Episcopal Church Winnemucca, Nev.
Soft cover
74-plus pages
Many ads. Recipes attributed to contributors
Value: $39-$69

New Hampshire, Jaffrey

1954
Personal Recipes Pilgrim Fellowship Of The Federated Church
Pilgrim Fellowship of the Federated Church
North American
Soft cover, plastic comb binding
42 pages
Chapter openings illustrated. Recipes attributed to contributors.
Cover shows historic church photos. A few local advertisements
and brief church history
Value: $35-$62

New Jersey

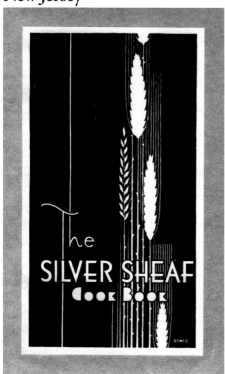

1930s
Silver Sheaf Cook Book
McClintock, Sara D.
Westfield District Nursing Association
Paperback
69 pages
Recipes attributed to contributors. Undated circa mid 1930s
Value: $31-$56

New York, Au Sable Forks

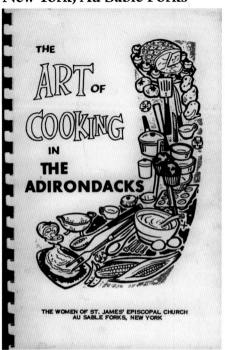

Circa 1960
Art Of Cooking In The Adirondacks, The
Women of St. James Episcopal Church
Paperback
93 pages
Recipes attributed to contributors. Local advertisements.
Undated circa 1960
Value: $14-$24

Oregon, Eugene

1938
University Of Oregon Mothers Cook Book
University of Oregon Mothers
James, Kern & Abbott
Soft cover, plastic comb binding
160 pages
Recipes attributed to contributors. Plastic comb or spiral binding. Local and national advertisements
Value: $52-$93

Oregon, Portland

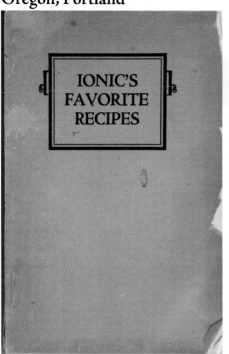

Circa 1915

Ionic's Favorite Recipes

Hurlburt, Frances E. (editor)

Ionic Court

Soft cover

77 pages

Oregon fundraiser charity cookbook by the Ionic Court Order of the Amaranth. Recipes attributed to contributors. Local advertisements. Undated circa 1915

Value: $49-$87

Pennsylvania, Clearfield

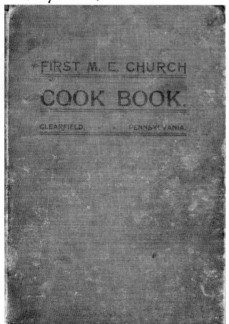

Circa 1903

First M. E. Church Cook Book

Methodist Episcopal Church, Clearfield, Pa.

Hardcover

84 pages

First Methodist Episcopal Church Cook Book, Clearfield, Pa. Undated circa 1903. Local advertisements

Value: $60-$106

South Carolina, Charleston

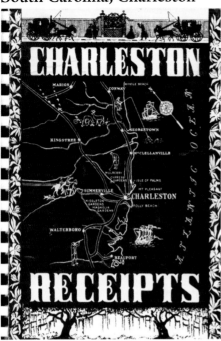

1950, 1978
Charleston Receipts
Charleston Junior League
Soft cover, Plastic Comb Bound
Enduring regional Junior League fundraising cookbook
originally printed in 1950
Recipes attributed to contributors
Value: $18-$31

Tennessee, Gatlinburg

1936
Pi Beta Phi Cook Book
Pi Beta Phi National Fraternity Members
Los Angeles Alumnae Club of Pi Beta Phi
Soft cover, wire bound
128 pages
Recipes attributed to and contributed by Pi Beta Phi
fraternity members (Settlement School in Gatlinburg, Tenn.)
around the country
Value: $36-$64

Texas, Greenville

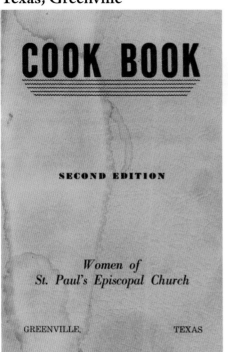

Circa 1950
Cook Book St. Paul's Episcopal Church Greenville, Texas
Women of St. Paul's Episcopal Church
Stapled booklet
74 pages
Local advertisements. Recipes attributed to contributors.
Undated circa 1950
Value: $32-$56

Texas, Houston

1968, 1992
Houston Junior League Cookbook 1968, 1992
Houston Junior League
Hardcover
432 pages
Reprinted in 1992. Original printing remains slightly more popular and is shown
Value: $18-$31

United States

The General Federation
of Women's Clubs
COOK BOOK

America COOKS

THE FIRST COMPLETELY NEW, MAJOR, ALL-PURPOSE COOK BOOK

TO APPEAR IN A GENERATION ☆ ☆ OVER 3,500 TESTED

RECIPES ☆ ☆ THE BEST RECIPES FROM THE TREASURED

PERSONAL FILES OF A MILLION AMERICAN COOKS

Edited by Ann Seranne

1967
America Cooks—General Federation Of Women's Clubs

Seranne, Ann (editor)

G. P. Putnam & Sons

Hardcover

796 pages

Long considered one of the most interesting and thorough charity foundation cookbooks

Value: $63-$112

Vermont, Burlington

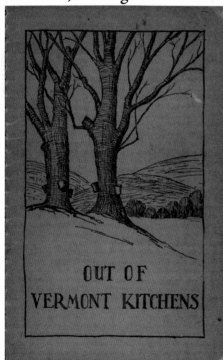

1939, 1944
Out Of Vermont Kitchens

Trinity Mission of Trinity Church

Trinity Mission Church

Soft cover, wire bound

400 pages

Many hand-drawn illustrations and all recipes written in the hand of the contributor and attributed to same. Local ads are hand-lettered and illustrated.

Early printings have wire binding, and later have plastic comb binding.

Value: $27-$48

Wisconsin, Milwaukee

1960

Treasured Recipes Beth El Ner Tamid Synagogue

Beth El Ner Tamid Synagogue
Paperback
268 pages
Revised 2nd edition. Includes holiday recipes and traditions
Recipes attributed to contributors
Value: $52-$93

CHARITY COOKBOOKS

The first known American charity cookbook, produced in 1864 as a fundraiser for the Union armies during the Civil War, was a cookbook written entirely in rhyme, titled *The Poetical Cook-Book*, compiled by Maria J. Moss.

Chapter 3:
Advertising Recipe Booklets

With the introduction of processed foods in the late 1800s, food manufacturers cooked up a new way to introduce their brands in a national marketplace: advertising pamphlets and booklets. Appliance and cookware manufacturers (mixers, refrigerators, stoves, pressure cookers, etc.) also found informative, inexpensive recipe booklets an effective way to instruct and inspire new users on the successful use of their products. For more than a century, these little publications have served as a mainstay promotional tool for introducing products and building brands old and new.

Booklets in this section are listed alphabetically by product name (for example, Crisco or Jell-O) or company name (for example, Heinz or Nestle). Because of their advertising and promotional nature, they tend to be visual and fun. Commonly designed by talented commercial artists, many are rich in the illustration, photography and color styles of the day.

Unlike conventional cookbooks, these booklets feature recipes related to, or created around a product—a paradigm rich in some creative concoctions one might not usually consider such as 7-UP Cheese Fondue (*Quick Recipe Favorites Distinctively Different with 7-UP*, 1965).

One of our favorites (and one we have trouble keeping in stock) is *Baker's Coconut Cut-up Cakes* (1956, promoting Baker's Angel Flake Coconut)—a little how-to booklet for wonderfully creative, animal and other fun-shaped cakes such as Coco the Nutty Clown, Quick-Like-A-Bunny and Mr. Snowman.

Following is just a small sampling of a vast category covering 150 years. Some are forgettable, many quite remarkable and a select part of them, we think, little works of art in themselves.

Armour

Circa 1944
Defense Of Health With Economy Meats
Gifford, Marie
Armour and Co.
Stapled booklet
36 pages
Wartime recipe booklet by Armour and Co.
36 pages with patriotic theme throughout
Undated circa 1944. Black-and-white photos
Value: $46-$81

Circa 1948
36 Thrifty Meals With Star Canned Meats
Gifford, Marie
Armour
Stapled booklet
24 pages
Appealing character chef illustrations throughout. Photo spread showing Armour meat product packaging
Undated circa 1948
Value: $17-$31

Aunt Jenny

L ike Betty Crocker and Martha Meade, Aunt Jenny was warm, inviting, friendly and entirely mythical. Created as the face of Lever Brothers Inc.'s Spry Vegetable Shortening (a competitor of Crisco), Aunt Jenny was invented by Spry as a marketing tool for its products. Plump, white haired, bespectacled and almost notoriously enthusiastic as both a speaker and writer, she was portrayed by actress Edith Spencer in print ads and on her radio show, the long-running broadcast soap opera titled *Aunt Jenny's Real Life Stories* (1937-1956). Inexplicably, her later 1952 portrait shows her as a sprightly young homemaker—it seems that pie and Spry are the elusive fountain of youth. (We wish.)

Her books and recipe guides, including *Aunt Jenny's Favorite Recipes* and *Aunt Jenny's Cookies Cookbook* (1952) were all ghost written by other authors, most likely Lever Brother employees. Appropriately, the recipes featured Spry's own vegetable shortening, fan letters and queries. Requests mailed to Aunt Jenny were actually answered by Louise M. Rafferty, a "cooking adviser" and employee of Lever Brothers company.

See Recipe Booklets: Spry.

Baker's Coconut and Chocolate

1924-1925
Choice Recipes
Walter Baker & Co.
Stapled booklet
64 pages
Chocolate and cocoa recipes by celebrated cooks including Fannie Merritt Farmer, Maria Parloa and Mrs. Rorer. Candy recipes by Mrs. Janet McKenzie Hill. Includes a brief history of chocolate, the company and the trademark
Color insert of packaging designs
Value: $24-$43

1932
Baker's Best Chocolate Recipes
General Foods
Stapled booklet
60 pages
Color illustrations. Brief history of Walter Baker Co. and story of "Le Belle Chocolatiere," the maiden that adorned Baker's packaging
Value: $9-$16

1948-1958
Baker's Favorite Chocolate Recipes
General Foods
Soft cover
112 pages
Color photos
Value: $13-$23

1956
Baker's Coconut Cut-Up Cakes
General Foods
Stapled booklet
28 pages
12 adorable shaped cakes, one for each month plus a couple of extras like "Fuzzy Fido" color photos
Value: $30-$53

1962-1965
Baker's Chocolate And Coconut Favorites
General Foods
Stapled booklet
64 pages
Undated circa 1965
Contains a few of the "cut-up cake" recipes
Color photos
Value: $10-$18

1968
Baker's Coconut & Chocolate Party Cut-Up Cakes
General Foods
Baker's
Stapled booklet
32 pages
Value: $28-$50

Ball

Originally the Wood Jacket Can Co., the Ball Brothers Glass Manufacturing Co. began manufacturing the popular home canning Ball Jar in 1884. The first *Ball Blue Book* came along in 1909. All of the recipe booklets are collected.

1949
Ball Blue Book Of Home Canning Preserving And Freezing Recipes
Ball Brothers
Stapled booklet
56 pages
Recipes, photos and directions for using Ball Jars
Color photos
Value: $16-$28

Battle Creek Food Co.

1920s
Healthful Living
Battle Creek Food Co.
Stapled booklet
65 pages
Undated 1920s. Highly illustrated with color drawings
Includes a brief history of the Battle Creek Sanitarium
Value: $32-$56

Borden

Circa 1920
Borden's Eagle Brand Book Of Recipes
Bordens
Stapled booklet
31 pages
Undated circa 1920
Pretty color illustrations throughout
Value: $18-$31

1942
This Is My Book Of Magic Recipes
Borden
Stapled booklet
22 pages
Borden recipe booklet featuring Elsie the Cow
Black-and-white photos
Value: $25-$44

1946
Borden's Eagle Brand Magic Recipes 1946
Borden
Stapled booklet
26 pages
Eagle Brand sweetened condensed milk promo booklet
Value: $9-$16

Calumet

Circa 1915
Reliable Recipes
Calumet
Stapled booklet
75 pages
Undated circa 1915
Value: $10-$18

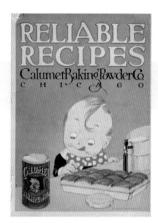

1916
Reliable Recipes
Calumet Baking Powder Co.
Stapled booklet
72 pages
Full page endorsement by Marion Cole Fisher includes her photo. Color illustration spread of Calumet Baking Powder Co. Color and black-and-white drawings of recipes throughout
Value: $20-$36

1931
Calumet Baking Book, The
General Foods
Stapled booklet
31 pages
Appealing color illustrations
Value: $16-$29

1934
Calumet Book Of Oven Triumphs, The
General Foods
Stapled booklet
32 pages
Black-and-white photos
Tear-out coupon for *All About Baking*
Value: $10-$18

Campbell

1941
Easy Ways To Good Meals: 99 Delicious Dishes Made With Campbell's Soups

Miller, Mary Ann
Campbell's Soup
Stapled booklet
48 pages
Color and black-and-white photos and illustrations. Photos of the Campbell test kitchens and home economists in action
Value: $5-$9

Circa 1950
Cooking With Condensed Soups

Marshall, Anne
Campbell Soup Co.
Stapled booklet
48 pages
Several appealing color illustrations of the Campbell Kids
Value: $9-$16

Carnation

1930
100 Glorified Recipes
Blake, Mary
Carnation Co.
Stapled booklet
36 pages
Very pretty illustrations grace this 1930s recipe booklet by Carnation.
Value: $15-$27

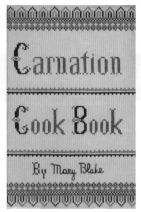

1935-1938
Carnation Cook Book
Blake, Mary
Carnation
Stapled booklet
93 pages plus index
Highly illustrated with color photos and spot color illustrations. Explanation of irradiated milk
Value: $12-$21

1939
Carnation Cook Book
Blake, Mary
Carnation
Stapled booklet
93 pages
Vivid color food photos and spot illustrations throughout Recipes feature Carnation "Irradiated" Milk.
Value: $10-$18

1948
Carnation Cook Book
Blake, Mary
Carnation
Soft cover
93 pages plus index
Essentially same recipes as earlier booklet, but different illustrations, photos and intro
Value: $12-$21

1951
Cook's Handbook, The
Blake, Mary
Carnation
Soft cover, plastic comb bound
96 pages
Color and black-and-white photos and illustrations
Value: $17-$31

Circa 1960
Carnation Cook Book
Carnation
Stapled booklet
24 pages
Undated circa 1960
Cover illustration signed "Butte." Appealing 1950s-'60s
graphic design and illustrations
Value: $10-$18

1955
Fun To Cook Book
Blake, Margie
Carnation Co.
Hardcover, plastic comb bound
48 pages
Cute illustrations and recipes. Reprinted many times through
the 1960s. Margie Blake is the fictional child of the equally
fictional Mary Blake.
Value: $20-$36

Ceresota Flour

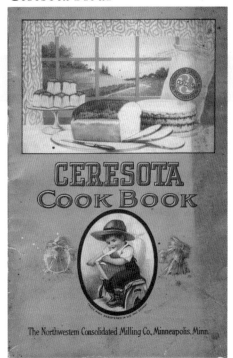

Circa 1910
Ceresota Cook Book
Ceresota Flour
Northwestern Consolidated Milling Co.
Stapled booklet
46 pages
Color illustrations. Promo recipe booklet for Ceresota Flour
Value: $33-$59

Clabber Girl

1934
Clabber Girl Baking Book
Hulman & Co.
Soft cover
Black-and-white illustrations
Value: $10-$38

Crisco

1937
Cooking Hints And Tested Recipes
Carter, Winifred S.
Proctor & Gamble
Stapled booklet
32 pages
Promotional recipe booklet for Crisco shortening.
Ad for *The Art of Cooking and Serving* (see Splint, Sarah Field) on the back cover. The book is available for 25 cents in stamps plus a wrapper from a can of Crisco.
Black-and-white photos
Value: $5-$8

Crocker, Betty

1932
15 Ways To A Man's Heart
Crocker, Betty
General Mills
Hardcover
24 pages
Small, stiff cover booklet
22 pages plus a tear-out coupon.
Large black-and-white photo of Betty Crocker on first page
Ad for Betty Crocker's New Recipe Box
Scarce
3 ½" x 5 ½"
Value: $21-$37

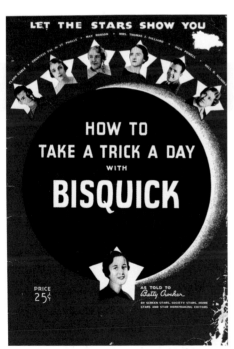

1935
How To Take A Trick A Day With Bisquick
Crocker, Betty
General Mills
Stapled booklet
41 pages
Clark Gable, Dick Powell, Bing Crosby, Joan Crawford, Bette Davis and many more 1930s stars contribute tips, recipes and menus. Photos of stars and table settings
Value: $25-$44

1943
Your Share
Crocker, Betty
General Mills
Stapled booklet
Wartime guide to preparing appetizing, healthful meals with "foods available today."
Many egg-less recipes and tips about how to get rations to go further
Very patriotic presentation and tone
Value: $21-$38

1950
Cooking For Fifty
Crocker, Betty
General Mills
Soft cover
34 pages
Value: $21-$37

Your favorites . . . with delicious pastry you can make so quickly using GOLD MEDAL "Kitchen-tested" Enriched Flour or Betty Crocker Homogenized Pie Crust Mix.

1955

All About Pie

Crocker, Betty
General Mills
Stapled booklet
16 pages
5-hole punched
Value: $12-$22

A treasury of favorite recipes modernized by Betty Crocker

1955

1880-1955 Gold Medal Jubilee Select Recipes

Crocker, Betty
Gold Medal Flour
Stapled booklet
Organized by century. Peppered with lots of historical food and company details
Highly illustrated
Value: $18-$31

1956
Betty Crocker's Bisquick Cook Book
Crocker, Betty
General Mills
Stapled booklet
26 pages
Value: $7-$12

1957
Betty Crocker's Bisquick Party Book
Crocker, Betty
General Mills
Stapled booklet
28 pages
Value: $4-$8

1957
Betty Crocker's Gold Medal Self-Rising Favorite Recipes
Betty Crocker
General Mills
Soft cover
32 pages
Value: $13-$22

1957
Betty Crocker's Softasilk Special Occasion Cakes
Betty Crocker
General Mills
Soft cover
31 pages
Value: $5-$9

1958
Betty Crocker's Country Kitchen Cookies
Crocker, Betty
General Mills
Stapled booklet
15 pages
Value: $9-$16

1959
133 Quicker Ways To Homemade ... With Bisquick
Crocker, Betty
General Mills
Stapled booklet
27 pages
Value: $3-$6

Diamond Walnuts

1935
To Win New Cooking Fame Just Add Walnuts
California Walnut Growers Assoc.
Stapled booklet
31 pages
Value: $10-$18

Circa 1935
For That Final Touch Just Add Diamond Walnuts
California Walnut Growers Assoc.
Stapled booklet
40 pages
Undated circa 1935
Last page is advertisement for a loose-leaf cookbook with index cards titled *Favorite Recipes*.
Value: $7-$12

Circa 1960
New Walnut Cook Book, The
Diamond Walnut Growers
Stapled booklet
28 pages
Undated circa 1960
Color and black-and-white photos and spot color illustrations
Value: $9-$16

Domino Sugar

1954
Keep Slim And Trim With Domino Sugar Menus
Author not noted
The American Sugar Refining Co.
Stapled booklet
24 pages
Cute period black-and-white illustrations. Color illustration of Domino packaging
Value: $9-$16

Dr. Pepper

1965
Cookin' With Dr. Pepper
Dr. Pepper
Stapled booklet
All recipes from Gingerbread to Hot Potato Salad use Dr. Pepper as an ingredient.
Value: $10-$18

Eatmor Cranberries

1930s

Cranberries And How To Cook Them
Eatmor Cranberries
American Cranberry Exchange
Stapled booklet
38 pages
Very charming graphics with the Eatmor Cranberry Man juggling, fencing, fishing, surfing, etc.
Many recipes and in-depth cranberry info
Color photos
Undated circa 1937
Value: $17-$31

Fleischmann

1962

Fleischmann Treasury Of Yeast Baking, The
Woods, Mary Lynn (editor)
Standard Brands Inc.
Stapled booklet
51 pages
Value: $9-$16

1968

Fleischmann's New Treasury Of Yeast Baking
Fleischmann
International Milling
Stapled booklet
34 pages
Value: $8-$15

Fruit Dispatch Co.

1940

Bananas ... How To Serve Them

Fruit Dispatch Co.
Stapled booklet
48 pages
56 recipes and an additional section with buying,
preparing and food-keeping information
Photos and amusing illustrations of dancing bananas
throughout
Value: $17-$31

General Electric

1951

General Electric Book Of Canning

General Electric
Stapled booklet
15 pages
Spot color illustrations
Value: $17-$31

General Foods

1939

Kate Smith's Favorite Recipes

Smith, Kate
General Foods
Stapled booklet
47 pages
Recipe booklet for Swans Down Flour and
Calumet Baking Powder using the promotional powers of
popular singer Kate Smith
Highly illustrated with black-and-white photos of Kate and
completed recipes
Value: $13-$23

1941

Cake Secrets

General Foods
Stapled booklet
60 pages
Cute promo cookbook for Swans Down and Calumet by
General Foods
Color and black-and-white photos and illustrations
Value: $11-$19

Circa 1944
Baking Secrets
General Foods
Stapled booklet
35 pages
Promotional booklet for Swans Down Flour
and Calumet Baking Soda brands. Includes
brief history of Swans Down flour
Black-and-white photos. Color illustrations
Undated circa 1944
Value: $10-$18

1945
Favorite Recipes For Country Kitchens
General Foods
Stapled booklet
45 pages
Dishes from across America using Calumet Baking Powder and
Swans Down flour
Black-and-white photos
Value: $11-$19

General Mills

1956
Cookies Galore
Barton, Frances
General Foods
Paperback
39 pages
Cute graphics and inventive and fun cookie ideas
using Post cereals
Black-and-white and color photos. Spot color illustrations
Value: $9-$16

1904, 1970
Gold Medal Flour Cook Book 1904
Christmas Edition
Washburn Crosby
General Mills
Paperback
72 pages
Facsimile reprint of an early Gold Medal Flour cookbook with
all manner of Christmas goodies
Value: $7-$12

Gettelman Milwaukee Beer

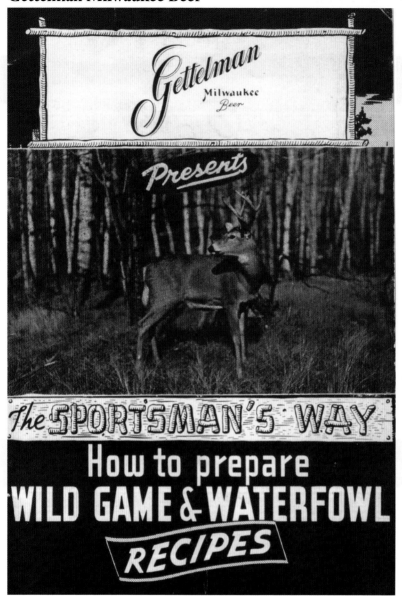

Circa 1940
Sportsman's Way, The: How To Prepare Wild Game & Waterfowl Recipes
Mills, Ruth Elizabeth
Gettelman Beer
Stapled booklet
64 pages
Undated circa 1940
Includes porcupine baked in clay and roast raccoon
Black-and-white drawings
Value: $30-$53

Ghirardelli Chocolate

Circa 1935
Sweet Sixteen Recipe Packet Number #3
Ghirardelli Chocolate
15 pages
Envelope and recipe cards
Undated circa 1935
Value: $15-$27

H. J. Heinz Co.

1930
Heinz Book Of Salads
Heinz
Stapled booklet
92 pages
Value: $6-$11

1956
Salads A Recipe Book By Heinz
H. J. Heinz
Stapled booklet
96 pages
Value: $5-$9

1957
57 Prize Winning Recipes
H. J. Heinz Co.
Stapled booklet
31 pages
Promo booklet from H.J. Heinz Co. Cook with Ketchup Contest
Color photos and cute dancing food illustrations
Value: $12-$21

Hershey

1934
Hershey's Index Recipe Book
Hershey
Stapled booklet
48 pages
Tabbed sections. Highly illustrated with color drawings of packaging and recipes
Value: $25-$45

1940
Hershey's Recipes
Hershey Chocolate Corp.
Stapled booklet
32 pages
Superior tinted food photos and airbrush illustrations. Middle spread shows product packaging.
Value: $25-$45

1971
Hershey's 1934 Cookbook
Hershey Chocolate
Hardcover, wire bound
96 pages
Reprint of the popular 1934 *Hershey's Index Recipe Book 1934* revised for modern kitchens
Value: $12-$21

Hotpoint

Hunt's

Circa 1945
Electric Cookery By Hotpoint
Edison General Electric Co., Inc.
Soft cover, wire bound
96 pages
Exceptional vintage graphics. Extensive photos of range. Color illustration of Mary Lowell Schwin, Hotpoint home economist
Undated circa 1945
Value: $14-$26

Circa 1965
21 New Ways To Serve Hamburger
Hunt's
Soft cover
23 pages
Undated circa 1965
Value: $6-$10

Jelke

1936
Jelke's Good Luck Recipes
Easton, Esther
John F. Jelke Co., Chicago
Soft cover, comb bound
64 pages
Promo cook booklet for the Jelke's Good Luck Vegetable Oleomargarine
Attractive design with many color and black-and-white photos and illustrations. Photo of the Jelke kitchen and of Esther Easton
Value: $18-$32

Jell-O

1916
Jell-O America's Most Famous Dessert
Genesse Pure Food
Stapled booklet
18 pages
Appealing miniature color paintings throughout. Hole-punched with string hanger
Value: $25-$44

1925
Jell-O Recipe Booklet (Train Cover)
Jell-O Co.
Stapled booklet
18 pages
Pretty little Jell-O promotional recipe booklet highly illustrated with detailed paintings
Additional advertisement envelope booklet for JELL-O Ice Cream Powder is tied in. Hole-punched with string hanger
Value: $20-$36

1931
Want Something Different?
General Foods
Stapled booklet
23 pages
Color illustrations of food and people
Value: $10-$18

Junket Rennet

1938
How To Make Rennet-Custards And Ice Cream
Junket Rennet
Stapled booklet
31 pages
Color and black-and-white photos
Value: $9-$16

Kellogg Co.

1937
Housewife's Year Book Of Health And Homemaking
Kellogg Co.
Soft cover
35 pages
Promotional booklet for Kellogg's products with recipes, historical, astrological, homemaking and other useful information
Adept color illustrations
Value: $16-$28

Kerr

1943
Kerr Home Canning Book
Kerr Glass
Stapled booklet
56 pages
Wartime edition of *Kerr Home Canning* instruction and recipe booklet
Color photos
Value: $17-$31

Knox Gelatine

1929
Knox Gelatine Dainty Desserts Candies Salads 1929
Knox
Stapled booklet
47 pages
Appealing color illustrations
Value: $5-$9

1957
Good Looking Cooking
Knox Gelatine
Stapled booklet
15 pages
"A guide to the use of unflavored gelatine for students"
Cute graphics and illustrations
Value: $9-$16

1963
Gel It!
Knox
Stapled booklet
15 pages
Cute promo recipe booklet by Knox with gels, party snacks, and diet and beauty tips
Spot color illustrations
Value: $6-$10

Kraft-Phenix Cheese

1936
Favorite Recipes From Marye Dahnke's File
Dahnke, Marye
Kraft-Phenix Cheese
Stapled booklet
46 pages
Includes Kraft's Macaroni and Cheese recipe here titled "Macaroni American"
Highly illustrated with exceptional food illustrations as well as small black-and-white 1930s-style spot illustrations. Several pages showing Kraft packaging. See also: General Cookbooks: Dahnke, Mary.
Value: $16-$28

Lea & Perrins

1935
Success In Seasoning
Lea & Perrins
Stapled booklet
47 pages
Black-and-white photos and illustrations
Value: $17-$31

1952
Dishes Men Like
Lea & Perrins
Stapled booklet
62 pages
Brief history of Lea & Perrins. A collection of recipes to "please a man"
Value: $12-$21

Majestic Mfg.

1898
Majestic Cook Book
Majestic Mfg.
Stapled booklet
96 pages
Recipes like Ginger Pudding, Dry Curing Bacon and Sweet Potato Croquettes. Additional section with helpful tips for getting rid of bedbugs and cleaning the range
Illustrations of many models and accessories, as well as specifications for many more
Undated circa 1898
Hole-punched with string hanger. Black-and-white illustrations
Value: $62-$102

Metropolitan Life

1929
Three Meals A Day
Metropolitan Life Insurance Co.
Stapled booklet
16 pages
Value: $6-$10

Circa 1935
Metropolitan Cook Book
Metropolitan Life Insurance Co.
Stapled booklet
64 pages
Undated circa 1935
Value: $8-$15

1957
Metropolitan Cook Book
Metropolitan Life
Stapled booklet
56 pages
Spot color illustrations
Value: $3-$6

Minute Tapioca

1934
Easy Triumphs With The New Minute Tapioca
General Foods
Stapled booklet
47 pages
Color illustrations
Value: $6-$11

Mirro

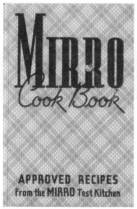

1937
Mirro Cook Book
Wilson, Laura
Aluminum Goods Mfg. Co.
Hardcover
284 pages
Shows large selection of Mirro utensils
Value: $13-$23

Morrell

1941
Treasured Recipes Of The Old South
Kimball, Marie Mrs.
John Morrell & Co.
Stapled booklet
20 pages
Promo cook booklet for Morrell Ham by the author of the *Thomas Jefferson Cookbook* and the *Martha Washington Cookbook*
Appealing color illustrations and Technicolor period photos
Value: $14-$25

Nestle

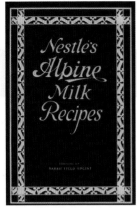

Circa 1920

Nestle's Alpine Milk Recipes

Splint, Sarah Field (editor)
Nestle Food Co.
Stapled booklet
24 pages
Embossed cover. Color illustrations
Undated circa 1920
Value: $13-$23

Oscar Mayer

1959

Oscar Mayer Cookout Fun

Oscar Mayer Co.
Stapled booklet
31 pages
Scarce promo booklet
Highly illustrated with period 1950s Technicolor photos of happy people, and wiener and ham recipes
Value: $20-$36

Pet Milk

1949

Husband-Tested Recipes From Mary Lee Taylor's Pet Milk Kitchen

Taylor, Mary Lee
Pet Milk
Stapled booklet
31 pages
Black-and-white photos and illustrations. Photo of Mary Lee Taylor
Two-hole punched
Value: $21-$38

COLLECTING TIP

Always of interest are the funny, the odd and the kitschy. Adding instant collector appeal are illustrations of dancing hot dogs, photos of ultra-happy housewives in pearls and high-heels, and recipes for kooky foods.

Pillsbury

1926
50 Prize Winning Recipes For Pillsbury's Health Bran
Pillsbury
Stapled booklet
16 pages
Recipes submitted by housewives in a nation-wide bran recipe contest
Value: $13-$23

1945-1946
Bake The No-Knead Way Ann Pillsbury's Amazing Discovery
Pillsbury
Stapled booklet
64 pages
Color and black-and-white photos and illustrations
Value: $20-$36

1948
Baking Is Fun!
Pillsbury, Ann
Pillsbury
Stapled booklet
64 pages
Printed in 1945-1948. 1948 third edition is revised to include a variety of new recipes.
Color photos. Additional tipped-in page with info about the Pillsbury Extra-Value Coupon Plan
Value: $16-$28

1950s
Short-Cut Breads
Pillsbury
Stapled booklet
40 pages
Undated
Five-hole punched
Value: $18-$31

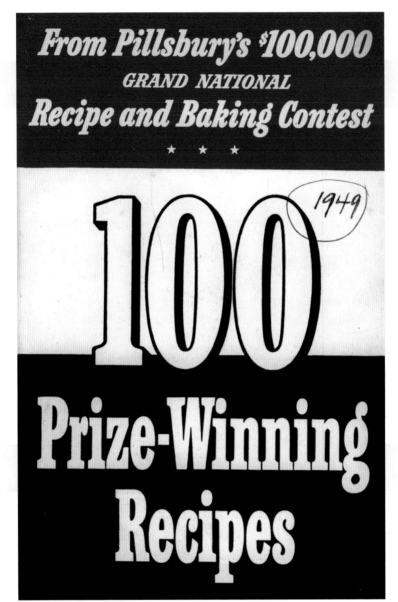

1950
100 Prize-Winning Recipes From Pillsbury's $100,000 Grand National Recipe and Baking Contest
Pillsbury, Ann
Pillsbury
Stapled booklet
96 pages
The 100 prize-winning recipes from the first Pillsbury Bake-Off contest on Dec. 13, 1949
Color and black-and-white photos
Value: $32-$56

1952
Kate Smith Chooses Her 55 Favorite Ann Pillsbury Cake Recipes
Pillsbury, Ann
Stapled booklet
64 pages
Especially created for Sno Sheen cake flour
Value: $12-$21

1958
Pillsbury Hot Roll Mix Baking Book
Pillsbury
Stapled booklet
65 pages
Five-hole punched
Color and black-and-white photos and illustrations
Value: $9-$16

Circa 1958
Fun Filled Butter Cookie Cookbook
Pillsbury
Stapled booklet
48 pages
Undated circa 1958
50 recipes from Ann Pillsbury's recipe exchange, including favorite Grand National Prize winners
Value: $10-$18

Circa 1958
Pillsbury's Best Butter Cookie Cookbook Volume 2
Pillsbury
Stapled booklet
50 pages plus coupons
Volume 2
Color and black-and-white photos and illustrations
Undated circa 1958
Value: $6-$11

Tangy Hawaiian Pie

Circa 1958
Pillsbury's Best Butter Cookie Cookbook Volume 3
Pillsbury
Stapled booklet
50 pages plus coupons
Five-hole punched
Recipes attributed to contributors
Undated circa 1958
Color and black-and-white photos and illustrations
Value: $12-$21

Circa 1960
Cool Ideas Cook Book
Pillsbury
Stapled booklet
32 pages
Undated circa 1960
Color and black-and-white photos
Five-hole punched
Value: $13-$23

Circa 1960
Fabulous Pies From Pillsbury
Pillsbury
Stapled booklet
24 pages
Five-hole punched
Undated circa 1960
Color and black-and-white photos and illustrations
Value: $16-$28

1960s
Best Loved Foods Of Christmas
Pillsbury
Stapled booklet
65 pages
65 recipes for America's hospitable holiday season featuring the 10 best butter cookies Five-hole punched
Undated circa 1960s
Value: $12-$21

Pyrex

1960s

Best Recipes Pillsbury Binder
Pillsbury
Binder
Hard-to-find Pillsbury binder with stand for *Best of the Bake-off* booklets
Binder price without contents
Value: $28-$50

1926

New Tests Prove That Foods Actually Bake Better This Way
Corning Glass
Stapled booklet
29 pages
Serves as a catalog and a recipe booklet showing uses and examples of Pyrex ovenware
Black-and-white photos and illustrations
Value: $20-$36

R.T. French

1953

Pyrex Prize Recipes
Pyrex
Greystone Press
Hardcover
128 pages
Photos and directions for use of Pyrex cookware along with recipes
Value: $28-$49

1951

Seasoning Makes The Difference
French, Carol
R. T. French Co.
Stapled booklet
31 pages
Color photos. Drawing of the fictional Carol French
Five-hole punched
Value: $17-$31

Ronrico

Circa 1935
Ronrico Chico's "A" To "Z"
Drink Guide
Ronrico
Stapled booklet
20 pages
Spot color illustrations
Value: $18-$31

COLLECTING TIP

Cocktail booklets continue to grow in popularity and are often collected for their colorful graphics and historic, period or lost recipes of interest among cocktail aficionados.

Roto-Broil Corp.

Roto-Broil, the cook-it-all appliance and forerunner of the toaster oven, was once so beloved and famous that Roy Lichtenstein, the mid-century pop artist, made it the subject of one of his paintings.

Circa 1955
Roto-Broil Custom 400
Roto Broil
Stapled booklet
15 pages
Complete recipes, directions, parts and diagrams for the Roto-broil Custom 400
Value: $31-$56

1955
Mr. & Mrs. Roto-Broil Cook Book
Revised Edition
Alexander, Sarah
Roto-Broil Corp.
Soft cover
255 pages
Value: $17-$31

Royal Baking Powder

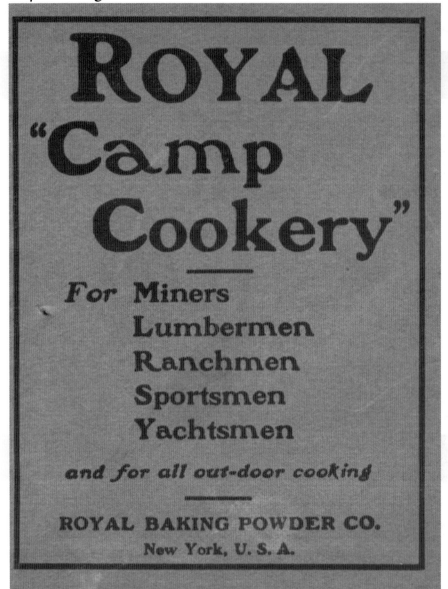

ROYAL "Camp Cookery"

For Miners
Lumbermen
Ranchmen
Sportsmen
Yachtsmen

and for all out-door cooking

ROYAL BAKING POWDER CO.
New York, U. S. A.

1910
Royal Camp Cookery
Kenealy, Capt. A. J.
Royal Baking Powder Co.
Stapled booklet
32 pages
Advertising or promotional recipe booklet by Royal Baking Powder Co.
"Specially prepared for use by Capt. A. J. Kenealy, the author of many articles and books on subjects of outdoor work and sport"
Scarce
Prepared as a promotional cookbook and recounts the success of the baking powder when used by contractors digging the Panama Canal, by miners in the South African Mines, by gold diggers of the Klondyke and Cape Nome and as the only brand that can stand the heat of the jungle and the cold of the Arctic
Value: $27-$48

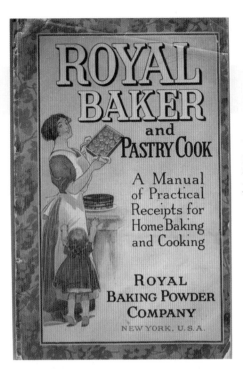

1911
Royal Baker And Pastry Cook
Royal Baking Powder Co.
Stapled booklet
44 pages
Value: $9-$16

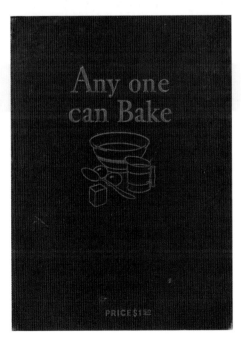

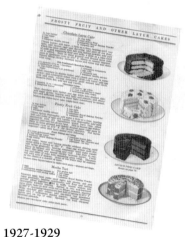

1927-1929
Any One Can Bake
Royal Baking Powder
Hardcover
100 pages
Step-by-step, black-and-white photos and lovely color
drawings of cakes and pastries
Includes the story of baking powder
Value: $18-$31

1928
Royal Cook Book
Royal Baking Powder
Stapled booklet
49 pages
Value: $9-$16

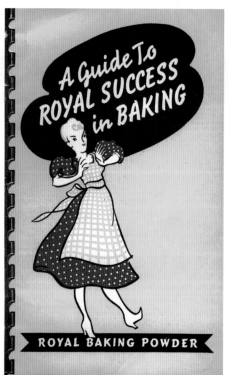

1940
Guide To Royal Success In Baking, A
Royal Baking Powder
Stapled booklet
22 pages
Includes the stories of baking powder and cream of tartar
Value: $9-$16

Royal Gelatin

1942
Royal Recipe Parade
Standard Brands
Soft cover
48 pages
Highly illustrated with color and black-and-white photos and
exceptional character drawings
Value: $25-$44

COLLECTING TIP

Look for booklets rich in
fun or interesting period
styles of drawing, painting
or artistic enhancement.
Many cookbooks were
illustrated by some of the
most creative commercial
artists of their time.

1913
Rumford Recipe Book
Farmer, Fannie; Wallace, Lily Haxworth; and Maddocks, Mildred
Rumford
Stapled booklet
24 pages
Advertising or promotional recipe booklet by Rumford
Lovely cover. No interior illustrations
Threaded for hanging
6" x 9 ⅛"
Value: $27-$48

1918
Rumford Cook Book
Farmer, Fannie Merritt
Rumford Co.
Stapled booklet
48 pages
Undated circa 1918
Hole with thread for hanging
Value: $11-$19

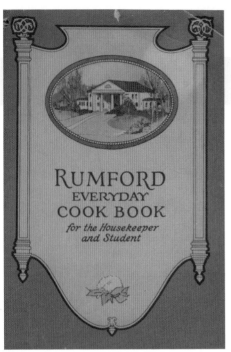

Circa 1918
Rumford Everyday Cook Book For The Housekeeper And Student
Wilson, Mary A.; Wallace, Lily Haxworth; and Hill, Janet Mckenzie
Stapled booklet
68 pages
Undated circa 1918
Hole-punched with string hanger
Value: $10-$18

Circa 1930
Rumford Common Sense Cook Book
Wallace, Lily Haxworth
Rumford
Stapled booklet
64 pages
Undated circa 1930
Value: $8-$14

Ryzon

1917
Ryzon Baking Book
Neil, Marion Harris
General Chemical Co.
Hardcover
81 pages
Promotional cookbook for Ryzon Baking Powder with terrific period color illustrations
A few of the prize-winning recipes include pineapple fritters, nut tart and a Rum Baba
Value: $24-$43

Santa Clara County Fruit Exchange

1905
California Prune, The
Santa Clara County Fruit Exchange
Mutual
Stapled booklet
24 pages
Scarce early California Prune promotional booklet with exceptional illustrations
Value: $32-$56

Seven-up

1961
7-Up Goes To A Party
Seven-Up Co.
Stapled booklet
14 pages
Value: $12-$21

1965
Quick Recipe Favorites
Distinctively Different With 7 Up
Seven-up
Stapled booklet
15 pages
Color and black-and-white photos and illustrations
Value: $6-$12

Snowdrift

1913
Snowdrift Secrets
Rorer, Sarah Tyson
Southern Cotton Oil Co.
Stapled booklet
46 pages
Advertising or promotional recipe booklet by Southern Cotton Oil Co. An early promo cook booklet example by Mrs. Rorer
Value: $12-$21

Sperry Flour

*Inside Page
Sample*

Circa 1945

60 Recipes For Making Good Things To Eat

Wesson Oil & Snowdrift People
Stapled booklet
28 pages
Also titled *The New Snowdrift Cook Book*. 1940s cook booklet from Wesson Oil and Snowdrift
Blue and black photos
Undated circa 1945
Value: $11-$19

1944

Stars Of Western Cookery Present A Round-Up Of Wartime Recipes, The

Meade, Martha
General Mills
Stapled booklet
12 pages
Nine popular home economists from west coast radio and newspapers present their favorite recipes. The economists: Mary Cullen, Dorothy Dean, Pauline Edwards, Nancy Finch, Ann Holden, Katherine Kitchen, Marian Manners, Dorothy Neighbors, Norma Young and the fictional Martha Meade.
Black-and-white photos of contributors
Value: $28-$49

1958
Martha Meade's Failure-Proof Recipes
Meade, Martha
Sperry
Stapled booklet
32 pages
Black-and-white photos and illustrations
Value: $6-$11

Spry

Circa 1935
What Shall I Cook Today?
Spry
Stapled booklet
48 pages
Desirable cook booklet promoting use of Spry vegetable shortening. Front and back cover in cartoon format
Undated circa 1935-1940
No mention of Aunt Jenny, but there are "Aunt Jane's Cookies"
Value: $11-$19

Circa 1940
Aunt Jenny's Favorite Recipes (Spry)
Lever Brothers
Stapled booklet
49 pages
Black-and-white photos of "Aunt Jenny" and her kitchen throughout
Undated circa 1940
Value: $12-$21

1942
Good Cooking Made Easy
Lever Brothers Co.
Stapled booklet
48 pages
Aunt Jenny Spry cook booklet
Color and black-and-white photos and illustrations
Value: $12-$22

1950

10 Cakes Husbands Like Best

Aunt Jenny
Spry
Soft cover
16 pages
Undated circa 1950
Value: $12-$21

1952

Aunt Jenny's 12 Pies Husbands Like Best Recipe Book

Aunt Jenny
Lever Brothers
Stapled booklet
20 pages
Value: $12-$21

1952

Aunt Jenny's Old-Fashioned Christmas Cookies

Aunt Jenny
Lever Bros.
Stapled booklet
21 pages
Value: $9-$16

1955

Spry 20th Anniversary Cookbook Of Old And New Favorites

Lever Brothers
Stapled booklet
25 pages
Black-and-white photos and illustrations
Value: $10-$18

Sun-Maid

Circa 1945
Downright Delicious Sun-Maid Raisin Recipes
Sun-Maid
Stapled booklet
32 pages
Charming early Sun-Maid recipe booklet including recipes for Waldorf Salad, Raisin Bran Muffins, Swedish Tea Ring, Scones, Apple Raisin Brown Betty, Hermits, Oregon Chess Pie and many more.
Undated circa 1940
Value: $10-$18

Sunbeam

1957
How To Get The Most Out Of Your New Deluxe Sunbeam Automatic Mixmaster
Sunbeam
Soft cover
42 pages
Instruction and recipe book shows attachments and care
Back cover shows Sunbeam products
Value: $11-$19

Sunkist

1940
Sunkist Fresh Grapefruit Recipes
Sunkist
Stapled booklet
18 pages
$6
Value: $11-$21

Swans Down

1942
Good Cooking Made Easy
Lever Brothers Co.
Stapled booklet
48 pages
Aunt Jenny Spry cook booklet
Color and black-and-white photos and illustrations
Value: $12-$22

1953
Cake Secrets
Barton, Frances (editor)
General Foods
Stapled booklet
64 pages
Color and black-and-white photos
Value: $12-$21

Underwood

1915
Good Tastes For Good Times
W.M. Underwood
Stapled booklet
30 pages
Includes a history of Underwood and photos of the Underwood Kitchen
Value: $21-$40

Circa 1935
Little Red Devil Recipes, The
Wm. Underwood
Stapled booklet
29 pages
Includes history of Underwood and Deviled Ham
Undated circa 1930s
Value: $16-$28

Washburn-Crosby

1917
Gold Medal Flour Cook Book
Washburn Crosby Co.
Washburn Crosby
Stapled booklet
74 pages
Hole-punched with hanging string
Title page title: *Washburn Crosby's Gold Medal Cook Book*
Coupons for additional books on pages 73-74. Spot tinted
illustrations. Some printings have an advertisement for Betty
Crocker's Recipe Box on page 73 instead of coupons.
Reprinted many times, with earlier versions being more desirable
Value: $28-$49

Wear-Ever

1929

Wear-Ever New Method Of Cooking And 100 Tested Recipes

Blake, Mary
Aluminum Cooking
Stapled booklet
48 pages
Many period illustrations of Wear-Ever cookware and food. Color and black-and-white illustrations
Value: $16-$28

1936

Wear-Ever New Method Of Cooking For Health For Flavor For Economy

Aluminum Cooking Utensil Co.
Stapled booklet
48 pages
Art Deco cover design with aluminum ink. Color and black-and-white illustrations of utensils, the company building and foods throughout
Value: $15-$27

COLLECTING TIP

Old appliance manuals aid in the use and repair of antique appliances, often containing product photos, assembly schematics and parts identification.

1937

Wear-Ever: New Method Cooking Instruction Book

Wear-Ever
Aluminum Cooking Utensil Co.
Stapled booklet
62 pages
Recipes and guide to using and caring for Wear-Ever products. Complete section showing all available Wear-Ever products and utensils. Color photos
Value: $9-$16

1946
Wear-Ever New Method Cooking Instruction Book
Aluminum Cooking Utensil Co.
Stapled booklet
64 pages
Instructions and recipes, highly illustrated with photos and drawings. Includes illustrations and identification of the cookware line
Value: $10-$18

1952
Wear-Ever New Method Cooking Instruction Book
Aluminum Cooking Utensil Co., The
Stapled booklet
96 pages
Instructional cookbook for use with Wear-Ever aluminum cookware. Shows parts and combinations of different cookware products. Black-and-white and color illustrations
Value: $5-$9

Wolfschmidt

1962
Wear-Ever New Method Cook Book
Mitchell, Margaret
Wear-Ever Aluminum Inc.
Soft cover
48 pages
Recipes for cooking with Wear-Ever utensils. Includes many pages of illustrations of utensils and food. Appealing vintage color photos, illustrations and graphic design throughout
Value: $11-$19

Circa 1955-1960
Wolfschmidt Vodka Instant Hospitality Party Book, The
Wolfschmidt Vodka
Stapled booklet
19 pages
Spot color illustrations
Undated circa 1955-1960
Value: $4-$7

Bibliography & Online Resources

Much of the research for this book was gleaned from the dust jackets and text of the actual cookbooks listed in the guide. In the case of company publications, official corporate websites were also consulted. Lynne Olver, editor and researcher at foodtimeline.org, provided additional research.

Other resources consulted to substantiate facts include corporate websites, past and recent newspaper articles, author biographies, food blogs and library projects. Please note that while every possible attempt at accuracy was made in the writing of this book, it is not intended as a substitute for academic research.

Allen, Col. Bob, *A Guide To Collecting Cookbooks and Advertising Cookbooks, A History of People, Companies and Cooking*. Paducah, Ky., Collector Books, 1990

Anderson, Jean, *The American Century Cookbook, The Most Popular Recipes of the 20th Century*. New York, N.Y., Clarkson Potter Publishers, 1997

Arndt, Alice, *Culinary Biographies*. Houston, Texas, YES Press, Inc., 2006

Barile, Mary, *Cookbooks Worth Collecting, The History and Lore of Notable Cookbooks, with Complete Bibliographic Listings and Up-to-date Values*. Radnor, Pa., Wallace-Homestead Book Co.

Better Homes and Gardens Books, *Better Homes and Gardens Golden Treasury of Cooking*. Meredith Corp., 1973

Bitting, Katherine, *Gastronomic Bibliography*. London, The Holland Press Limited, 1981

Brown, Eleanore and Bob, *Culinary Americana, 100 Years of Cookbooks Published in the United States from 1860-1960*. Roving Press, 1961

Daniels, Frank, *Collector's Guide To Cook Books, Identification & Values*. Paducah, Ky., Collector Books, 2005

DuSablon, Mary Anna, *America's Collectible Cookbooks*. Athens, Ohio, Ohio University Press, 1994

Hale, William Harlan and the editors of *Horizon Magazine*, *The Horizon Cookbook and Illustrated History of Eating and Drinking Through The Ages*. American Heritage Publishing Co., Inc., Doubleday & Co., Inc., 1968

Herman, Judith and Herman; and Shalett, Marguerite, *The Cornucopia, Being A Kitchen Entertainment And Cookbook*. New York, N.Y., Harper & Row, Publishers, 1973

Lowenstein, Eleanor, *Bibliography of American Cookery Books 1742-1860*. Worcester, Mass., The Heffernan Press, Inc.

Norman, Sandra J. and Andes, Karrie K., *Vintage Cookbooks and Advertising Leaflets*. Atglen, Pa., Schiffer Publishing Ltd., 1998

Stage, Sarah and Vincenti, Virginia B., *Rethinking Home Economics, Women and the History of a Profession*. Ithaca, N.Y., Cornell University Press, 1997

Tannahill, Reay, *Food In History, the New, Fully Revised and Updated Edition of the Classic Gastronomic Epic*. New York, N.Y., Crown Publishers, Inc. 1988

Sunset Magazine, A Century of Western Living 1898-1998, Historical Portraits and A Chronological Bibliography of Selected Topics. Stanford, Calif., Stanford University Libraries, 1998

ONLINE RESOURCES

Feeding America: The Historic American Cookbook Project, Michigan State University Libraries: http://digital.lib.msu.edu/projects/cookbooks
www.epicurious.com
www.foodtimeline.org
www.IWFS.org (International Wine and Food Society)
www.jamesbeard.org
www.museum.tv
www.oldcookbooks.com
www.whitehousehistory.org

Alphabetical Title Index

More Kitchen and Cookery Collectibles Expertise

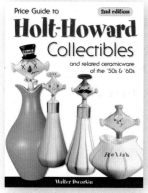